The STARVING STUDENTS' Cookbook

REVISED EDITION

by Dede Hall

Illustrations by Rob Sterling

WARNER BOOKS

A Time Warner Company

Warner Books, Inc. 1271 Avenue of the Americas, New York, NY 10020
Visit our Web site at http://warnerbooks.com

 A Time Warner Company

Printed in the United States of America

First Printing: August 1994

10 9

Library of Congress Cataloging-in-Publication Data
Hall, Dede.
    The starving students' cookbook / Dede Hall ; illustrated by Rob
Sterling. — Rev. ed.
      p.   cm.
    Includes index.
    ISBN 0-446-39530-7
    1. Low budget cookery.   I. Title
TX652.H327 1994   93-30494
641-5'51—dc20   CIP

Cover design and illustration by Carmine Vecchio, Anagram Design Group Inc., New York

Have you ever burned your hand making popsicles?
Do you think Al Dente invented spaghetti?

Since 1983, ***The Starving Students' Cookbook*** has allayed the fears of even the most reluctant chefs. If cooking delicious, inexpensive meals and snacks with easy preparation and practically no clean-up sounds good to you, this is the only book you'll ever need. Before you know it, you'll be making:

- Pasta with Pesto
- Eggs Foo Yung
- Spinach Mandarin Salad
- Tequila Soaked Fish
- Curried Chicken
- Beef Mexicana

These delicious creations plus over a hundred more will make your ventures into the kitchen happy ones. You'll never know how you lived without it.

"The instructions are so understandable and easy that any non-cook can make meals in minutes."
—Forecast

❀ ❀ ❀

"One of the most elementary cookbooks ever devised . . . this time and money saver can help inspire eating habits and nutrition for college students."
—Changing Times

❀ ❀ ❀

"Although geared for the college crowd, *The Starving Students' Cookbook* is useful for anyone who doesn't want to cook and doesn't want to learn to cook, but does want to eat."
—Blade-Citizen, **San Diego County**

❀ ❀ ❀

THE STARVING STUDENTS' COOKBOOK

TO BOBBY,
THIS ONE'S FOR YOU

TABLE OF CONTENTS:

COLLEGE STUDENTS!

Living on your own and trying to cut college costs is great, but why didn't someone tell you what a PAIN cooking for yourself can be? Now, at last, a way to ease your misery—a cookbook just for you with recipes that are EASY to follow, QUICK to make, 1 or 2 servings, LOW COST, and above all, GREAT TASTING!!

THE STARVING STUDENTS' COOKBOOK would probably make a gourmet cook shudder. This book is filled with recipe directions such as "splash," "squirt," "handful," even a "plop" or two. These descriptions are used simply to make cooking time faster and easier and won't change the good taste of the food.

You probably get your fill of studying every day and the last thing you want to do is "study" a cookbook. Wouldn't you like to have meals that taste good without having to work at it? Even if you have never cooked before, you can now.

THE STARVING STUDENTS' COOKBOOK is written just for YOU!

THE EATING RIGHT PYRAMID

The U.S. Department of Agriculture recently publicized this visual guide in order to help the public become more aware of healthy choices in selecting their daily meals. The USDA's Dietary Guidelines state: "Each of these food groups provides some, but not all, of the nutrients you need. No one food group is more important than another; for good health, you need them all."

WHAT COUNTS AS 1 SERVING?

The amount of food that counts as 1 serving is listed below. If you eat a larger portion, count it as more than 1 serving. For example, a dinner portion of spaghetti would count as 2 or 3 servings of pasta.

Be sure to eat at least the lowest number of servings from the five major food groups listed at the right. You need them for the vitamins, minerals, carbohydrates, and protein they provide. Just try to pick the lowest fat choices from the food groups. No specific serving size is given for the fats, oils, and sweets group because the message is USE SPARINGLY.

FOOD GROUPS

Milk, Yogurt, and Cheese

1 cup of milk or yogurt	1½ ounces of natural cheese	2 ounces of process cheese

Meat, Poultry, Fish, Dry Beans, Eggs, and Nuts

2–3 ounces of cooked lean meat, poultry, or fish	1/2 cup of cooked dry beans, 1 egg, or 2 tablespoons of peanut butter count as 1 ounce of lean meat

Vegetable

1 cup of raw leafy vegetables	1/2 cup of other vegetables, cooked or chopped raw	3/4 cup of vegetable juice

Fruit

1 medium apple, banana, orange	1/2 cup of chopped, cooked, or canned fruit	3/4 cup of fruit juice

Bread, Cereal, Rice, and Pasta

1 slice of bread	1 ounce of ready-to-eat cereal	1/2 cup of cooked cereal, rice, or pasta

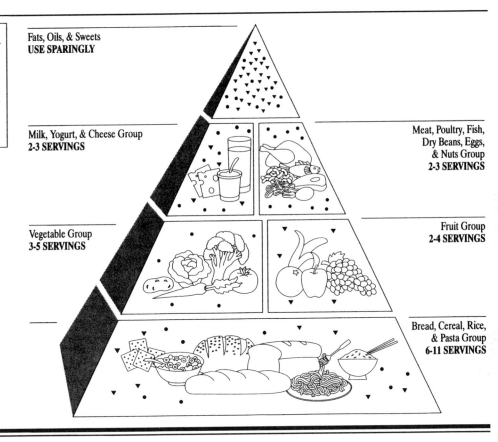

Key

● Fat (naturally occurring and added)
▼ Sugars (added)

These symbols show fat and added sugars in foods. They come mostly from the fats, oils, and sweets group. But foods in other groups—such as cheese or ice cream from the milk group or french fries from the vegetable group—can also provide fat and added sugars.

Fats, Oils, & Sweets
USE SPARINGLY

Milk, Yogurt, & Cheese Group
2-3 SERVINGS

Meat, Poultry, Fish, Dry Beans, Eggs, & Nuts Group
2-3 SERVINGS

Vegetable Group
3-5 SERVINGS

Fruit Group
2-4 SERVINGS

Bread, Cereal, Rice, & Pasta Group
6-11 SERVINGS

SHOPPING TIPS & KITCHEN HINTS

IN THE SUPERMARKET:
Check prices against weight to find the best buy.

Buy small quantities when cooking for one. Large "economy size" is no bargain when you have to throw away spoiled food.

Buy fruit and vegetables in season; they'll cost less and taste better.

NEVER buy or use canned goods that have "puffed out" ends, as this is a sign gas has built up within the can, which could produce a potentially deadly toxin.

Do your marketing after you have eaten. You'll buy less "junk food" and spend a lot less money.

For sweeter, juicier oranges, look for smoother skin and heavier weight.

Large size in fruit and vegetables doesn't always mean quality.

When head lettuce is too costly, try using some of the various leafy types. You'll be pleased at how delicious they are.

IN THE KITCHEN:

Keep fish in a tightly covered container to avoid a fishy smell throughout your refrigerator.

Roll lemons until slightly soft before squeezing. You will get a lot more juice out of them.

To chop onions without tears, hold a piece of bread partway in your mouth.

A paper towel in the bottom of the refrigerator vegetable drawer will keep the drawer clean and absorb food moisture.

Don't pour cold water into hot aluminum or stainless steel pans, it could cause them to warp out of shape.

Chopped apples, pears and bananas won't get discolored if you squeeze a bit of lemon juice on them.

Don't forget: When using the garbage disposal, run a strong flow of cold water through it at the same time to prevent drain blockage.

Adding a few grains of rice to salt keeps moisture from forming in shaker and helps salt to flow freely.

BASIC SUPPLIES TO GET YOU COOKING

BASIC UTENSILS:

Fry Pan (Skillet) and Lid
Plastic Bowl Set (with lids)
Pancake Turner (Spatula)
Glass Baking Dish (rectangle)
Large Ovenproof Pan and Lid
Saucepan with Lid

Aluminum Foil
Measuring Spoons
Sharp Knife
Glass Measuring Cup
Wooden Spoons
Scissors (to cut open stubborn packaging)

Don't Forget . . . Knife, Fork, Spoon and a Can Opener!

BASIC INGREDIENTS: What to buy and Where to find it in the supermarket

DAIRY CASE (always check freshness date):

Eggs, Milk, Sour Cream, Margarine, Cheddar Cheese, Orange Juice

CONDIMENTS:

Catsup, Mayonnaise, Mustard, Salad Dressing, Vegetable Oil, Vinegar, Lemon Juice, Barbecue Sauce, Soy Sauce

BAKING PRODUCTS AND SPICES:

Salt, Pepper, Sugar (granulated, brown), Garlic Powder or Salt, Flour, Herbs and Spices: Basil, Dill Weed, Parsley, Curry Powder, Paprika

CANNED VEGETABLES AND FRUIT:
    Beans (refried, chili, pork & beans), Cup-up Tomatoes, Corn, Pear Halves, Peach Slices

SAUCES, SOUPS AND GRAVY:
    Beef Gravy, Dry Onion Soup Mix, Tomato Sauce, Soup (condensed style); Cream of Mushroom, Tomato, Chicken Noodle

MACARONI, RICE AND MEAT PRODUCTS:
    Macaroni, Pasta, Rice (preferably not instant), Tuna

BREAD PRODUCTS AND SNACKS:
    Bread (your choice), Jelly or Jam, Peanut Butter, Pudding, Gelatin (Jell-O), Crackers, Cookies, Popcorn, Chips

These items will be useful if you have space in your refrigerator.

FRESH PRODUCE:
    Fruit (in season), Carrots, Celery, Potatoes, Onions, Nuts

MEAT CASE:
    Hot Dogs, Fish Fillets, Ground Beef (hamburger), Chicken

FROZEN FOOD (if you have freezer space):
    Ice Cream or Frozen Yogurt, Chopped Spinach, Broccoli Spears, Peas

Know how to tell a hard-cooked egg from a raw one?
The hard-cooked will spin like crazy.

Add a little vinegar to water when boiling eggs to prevent eggs from cracking.

BASICALLY BREAKFAST

1. FRIED:

(1) Heat butter in skillet on medium high heat till sizzles.
(2) Break eggs gently into skillet.
(3) Reduce heat to medium. Then:
- SUNNY SIDE UP—cook just till whites are set.
- BASTED—add spoonful water to pan, cover and let steam 2 minutes.
- OVER EASY—when whites are set; gently flip over with pancake turner.

2. SCRAMBLED:

(1) Break eggs into bowl; beat with fork lightly.
(2) Heat butter in skillet on medium high heat till sizzles. Pour eggs in.
(3) Reduce heat to medium low. Cook and stir gently till done to your liking.

3. SOFT-COOKED:

(1) Place eggs (with shells on) in saucepan. Add enough water to cover eggs. Set pan on stove and set heat at high.
(2) When water begins to boil rapidly, start timing eggs: 3 minutes for medium-done soft-cooked egg.
(3) Crack shell at large end of egg and remove shell. Eat from shell or scoop into a small bowl.

4. HARD-COOKED:

(1) Same as for soft-cooked, except boil 10 minutes.
(2) Turn off heat and let eggs sit in pan till water is cooled.

EGGS—THE WAY YOU LIKE THEM

5 MIN.

1 SERVING

BASICALLY BREAKFAST

SKILLET TOP OF STOVE

MEDIUM TO LOW HEAT

OMELET FILLINGS & TOPPINGS

1 TO 2 MIN.

BASICALLY BREAKFAST

MISC. UTENSILS

- Scoop of HOT CHILI and handful grated CHEESE
- Handful finely chopped HAM and SWISS CHEESE
- Sliced AVOCADO, finely chopped TOMATO and GREEN BELL PEPPER
- MUSHROOMS, lightly cooked in margarine in skillet
- Spoonful SOUR CREAM and chopped PARSLEY
- Grated CHEESE, spoonful BARBECUE SAUCE and ALFALFA SPROUTS
- Crumbled BACON, sliced BANANA

Be creative with your own combinations!!

NEED:

   3 EGGS
   2 tablespoons MILK
   dash SALT
   tablespoon MARGARINE

STEP 1: In bowl, mix together eggs, milk and salt.

STEP 2: In skillet, on medium heat, melt margarine. Add egg mixture. As eggs cook on edges, gently lift edges with spatula (flat spoon), pushing to center. Rest of uncooked egg will flow underneath cooked part. Do not stir, or you will have scrambled eggs.

STEP 3: When eggs are done to liking and surface is still moist, put any filling you want onto half of omelet and fold over. Cover with lid and cook 1 to 2 minutes or till eggs are golden on underside.

OMELET

10 MIN.

1 SERVING

BASICALLY BREAKFAST

SKILLET WITH LID
TOP OF STOVE

MEDIUM HEAT

5

FRENCH TOAST

10 MIN.

1 SERVING

BASICALLY BREAKFAST

PIE PAN & SKILLET
TOP OF STOVE

MEDIUM HIGH HEAT

NEED:
    4 slices BREAD (couple days old)
    2 EGGS
    2 tablespoons MILK
    2 tablespoons MARGARINE

STEP 1: Mix eggs and milk in pie pan.

STEP 2: In skillet, on medium high heat, heat margarine till hot. Dip bread slice into egg mixture, then lay onto hot skillet.

STEP 3: Cook each side till golden.

footnote: Top with syrup, applesauce, powdered sugar or fresh fruit.

NEED:
PACKAGED PANCAKE MIX (e.g., Bisquick)
SOUR CREAM or COTTAGE CHEESE
BERRIES, fresh, frozen (thawed) or canned (drained)
couple spoonfuls GRANULATED SUGAR

STEP 1: Using directions on package, prepare thin pancakes. Cook as directed making two or three large-size pancakes, being careful when you turn them. Set cooked pancakes on an attractive serving plate.

STEP 2: Spread spoonfuls of sour cream (or cottage cheese) along center of each pancake. Top with spoonful of berries and sprinkle of sugar.

STEP 3: Roll up each pancake and top with a few more berries, a small spoonful of sour cream (or cottage cheese) and small sprinkle of sugar.

footnote: Try this for a gorgeous dessert or impressive brunch!!

WHAT A CREPE

10 MIN.

SEVERAL SERVINGS

BASICALLY BREAKFAST

SKILLET
TOP OF STOVE

MEDIUM HIGH HEAT

HANDY HINT

Let's see: The big spoon is the Tablespoon
The little spoon is the Teaspoon

QUICK LUNCH

NEED:
   4 ENGLISH MUFFINS, cut in half
   1 8 oz. can TOMATO SAUCE
   Thin slices of any of the following:
   ONION, GREEN BELL PEPPER, MUSHROOMS, OLIVES, PEPPERONI,
   ANCHOVIES, SALAMI
   8 slices MOZZARELLA CHEESE

Preheat oven to 350°

STEP 1: Spread each half English muffin with tomato sauce.

STEP 2: Add slices of any combination from above ingredients, ending
   with cheese on top.

STEP 3: Place on foil in 350° oven till cheese melts.

ENGLISH MUFFIN PIZZAS

15 MIN.

2 TO 3 SERVINGS

QUICK LUNCH

ALUMINUM FOIL

350° OVEN

GREEK PITA BREAD FILLING

5 MIN.

1 SERVING

SMALL BOWL

NO COOKING

Combine in small bowl, then spread in pita bread pocket:
1/2 of 3-ounce pkg. CREAM CHEESE
1 tablespoon SOUR CREAM

Next, fill pocket with:
LETTUCE, shredded
1 TOMATO, thinly sliced
CHOPPED BLACK OLIVES (spoonful)
FETA or RICCOTA CHEESE (couple spoonfuls)
sliced BANANA

NEED:

- 3/4 cup BROWN SUGAR
- 2 cups FLOUR
- 3 teaspoons BAKING POWDER
- 3/4 cup chopped WALNUTS
- 1 EGG
- 2 teaspoon SALT
- 1 cup MILK
- 1 teaspoon OIL or MARGARINE (to grease loaf pan)

Preheat Oven to 350°

STEP 1: Dump all ingredients into mixing bowl and mix with wooden spoon till large lumps are gone.

STEP 2: Spoon into a greased loaf pan and bake in 350° oven about 50 minutes or till golden brown.

STEP 3: Remove from oven and set on wire rack (if you don't have a wire rack, use a couple of knives laid flat). Let cool before slicing.

footnote: Fabulous spread with margarine or cream cheese.

MOM'S NUT BREAD

1 HOUR

SEVERAL SERVINGS

QUICK LUNCH

SMALL LOAF PAN

350° OVEN

13

QUICK SANDWICH SPREADS

3 MIN.

1 SERVING

SMALL BOWL

NO COOKING

14

- **CARROT & PEANUT BUTTER**
1/4 cup PEANUT BUTTER
1 tablespoon SUNFLOWER SEEDS, shelled
1 tablespoon RAISINS
1 small CARROT, shredded
1 teaspoon CREAM CHEESE, softened

Mix in small bowl and spread on bread or toast.

- **EGG & OLIVE**—Mix together:
2 HARD-COOKED EGGS, chopped
1 1½ oz. can CHOPPED BLACK OLIVES
1 teaspoon SWEET PICKLE RELISH
1 tablespoon MAYONNAISE
Good on egg bread

- **PEANUT BUTTER, SLICED BANANAS, HONEY**
Spread wheat bread with butter, honey and peanut butter. Lay bananas in middle.

- **CHEESE & ONION**
1/2 ONION, thinly sliced
splash VINEGAR
dash PEPPER
SHARP CHEDDAR CHEESE, sliced

Lay onion in small bowl and sprinkle with vinegar and pepper. Let sit for a couple of minutes to blend flavors. Butter bread and layer with sliced cheese and onions.

- **CREAM CHEESE & PINEAPPLE**—Mix together:
3 oz. pkg. CREAM CHEESE, softened
1 tablespoon CRUSHED PINEAPPLE, well drained
1 teaspoon SUNFLOWER SEEDS

Good on raisin bread

QUICK LUNCH

SMALL BOWL

NO COOKING

WIENERS WITH GERMAN POTATOES

10 MIN.

1 TO 2 SERVINGS

SKILLET WITH LID TOP OF STOVE

LOW HEAT

NEED:
  1 15½ oz. can GERMAN-STYLE POTATOES
  4 WIENERS

STEP 1: Place wieners and potatoes in skillet.

STEP 2: Cover and heat on low till wieners puff and potatoes are hot.

STEP 3: At this time to improve taste add any, or all, of the following:
  • HARD-COOKED EGGS, sliced
  • BACON, crispy fried and crumbled
  • GREEN ONION, sliced
  • squirt VINEGAR, if you like it sour

Heat 1 minute. Serve.

Low-Cal Cocktail . . . Beef broth over ice with a "swizzle stick" of celery

Cleaning Lettuce: Remove core by tapping it sharply on hard surface. Core will come out easily. Then hold lettuce upside down under cold running water. Cleans and separates leaves at the same time.

SOUPS & SALADS

NEED:

4 slices BACON, cut up before cooking
1 GREEN ONION, sliced thin
1 8 oz. can CREAM-STYLE CORN
1 can CREAM OF MUSHROOM SOUP
1 soup can MILK
1 raw POTATO, cut into 1/2 inch cubes
1 6 oz. can MINCED CLAMS and juice

STEP 1: In saucepan, on medium heat, cook bacon till almost crisp. Add onion. Cook 1 more minute. Carefully drain grease into an old can. (Discard grease later when solidified.)

STEP 2: In same pan, add rest of ingredients. Bring to a boil. Reduce heat to low. Cover. Cook, stirring often, till potatoes are done (approximately 15 minutes).

FULL MEAL CLAM CHOWDER

20 MIN.

2 TO 3 SERVINGS

SOUPS & SALADS

**SAUCEPAN WITH LID
TOP OF STOVE**

**MEDIUM TO LOW
HEAT**

LATE NIGHT CHICKEN SOUP

20 MIN.

1 SERVING

SOUPS & SALADS

SAUCEPAN TOP OF STOVE

MEDIUM TO LOW HEAT

NEED:
- 1 10 oz. can CHICKEN BROTH
- 1 soup can WATER
- 2 teaspoons UNCOOKED RICE (not instant)
- 1 EGG
- 1 teaspoon LEMON JUICE

STEP 1: On medium high heat, into saucepan pour chicken broth, water and rice. Bring to boil. Turn heat down to lowest setting. Cook 20 minutes.

STEP 2: Just before serving, beat egg with lemon juice and pour into soup. Stir with fork and cook 1 minute on lowest setting. Serve while hot.

footnote: When you are up all night studying, try this instead of coffee to pep you up.

NEED:

    1/2 ONION, chopped small
    1 tablespoon MARGARINE
    2 medium POTATOES, peeled and chopped small
    1/2 cup WATER
    1 cup NONFAT MILK (not powdered)
    SALT, PEPPER to taste

STEP 1: In saucepan, on high heat, cook onion in hot margarine till limp (approximately 2 minutes).

STEP 2: Add potatoes and water. Boil gently 15 minutes or till potatoes are soft. Mash potatoes with fork while still in water. Do not drain!

STEP 3: Add milk, salt and pepper. Reduce heat to low and cook till hot, stirring often.

POTATO SOUP

18 MIN.

1 TO 2 SERVINGS

SOUPS & SALADS

SAUCEPAN
TOP OF STOVE

HIGH TO LOW HEAT

23

QUICK MINESTRONE SOUP

15 MIN.

1 TO 2 SERVINGS

**SAUCEPAN WITH LID
TOP OF STOVE**

**MEDIUM TO LOW
HEAT**

24

NEED:
1 tablespoon VEGETABLE OIL
1 ZUCCHINI, chopped
handful leftover COOKED MEAT, chopped small
1 16 oz. can WHOLE TOMATOES, cut up
1 8 oz. can GREEN BEANS (or 1 cup any leftover vegetables)
1 can WATER (use empty tomatoes can)
1/2 envelope DRY ONION SOUP MIX
small handful UNCOOKED MACARONI (small elbow)

STEP 1: In saucepan, on medium heat, heat oil and stir in zucchini and meat. Cook 2 minutes.

STEP 2: Add tomatoes, green beans and water. Bring to a boil.

STEP 3: Stir in onion soup mix and macaroni. Cover and cook 10 minutes on low heat.

footnote: Very filling. Great on a cold night.

SALAD #1
NEED:

  1/2 CUCUMBER, peeled and chopped
  3 tablespoons PLAIN YOGURT
  dash each of GARLIC SALT, PEPPER
  1/4 HEAD LETTUCE, shredded

Blend first 3 ingredients together in small bowl and serve over shredded lettuce.

SALAD #2
NEED:

  1/2 CUCUMBER, peeled and sliced thin
  1/2 small RED ONION
  1/2 cup SOUR CREAM
  quick squirt VINEGAR
  dash each of GARLIC SALT, PEPPER

Mix all ingredients together in small bowl. Chilling before eating improves the flavor.

SMALL BOWL

NO COOKING

3
SALAD
DRESSINGS

3 MIN.

**SMALL BOWL OR
JAR WITH TIGHT LID**

NO COOKING

- **ITALIAN**—Mix together and toss with salad:
2 tablespoons VEGETABLE OIL
1 tablespoon VINEGAR or LEMON JUICE
1 small CLOVE GARLIC, mashed
dash each of SALT, PEPPER
pinch OREGANO

1 serving

- **FRUIT SALAD**—Stir together in small bowl:
2 tablespoons MAYONNAISE or SOUR CREAM
1 teaspoon ORANGE JUICE (or juice from any canned fruit you may use)
SUGAR, to taste
Gently toss with fruit

1 serving

- **LEMON & OIL**—Shake together in jar with tight-fitting lid:
1/2 cup VEGETABLE OIL
1/3 cup LEMON JUICE
1 tablespoon SUGAR
dash SALT
1 teaspoon PAPRIKA
Makes enough salad dressing for several salads.

NEED:

2 TOMATOES, thinly sliced
1/2 small RED ONION, thinly sliced
SALT, PEPPER to taste
1/2 teaspoon DRY BASIL
1 tablespoon WINE VINEGAR
3 tablespoons OLIVE OIL (or VEGETABLE OIL)

STEP 1: In shallow platter, layer tomato and onion slices. Sprinkle with salt, pepper and basil. Pour vinegar and then oil over salad.

STEP 2: Let salad sit for at least 10 minutes to allow flavors to blend.

FRESH TOMATO SALAD

10 MIN.

1 TO 2 SERVINGS

SOUPS & SALADS

SHALLOW PLATE OR PLATTER

NO COOKING

GREEKS' FAVORITE WHOLE-MEAL SLAW

5 MIN.

1 TO 2 SERVINGS

LARGE BOWL

NO COOKING

NEED:
1/2 bag preshredded CABBAGE SLAW MIX
1 4 oz. can CHOPPED BLACK OLIVES, drained
handful WALNUTS, chopped
1 6½ oz. can MINCED CLAMS, well drained
couple spoonfuls RAISINS
SALT, PEPPER to taste
1 cup MAYONNAISE
1 tablespoon VINEGAR (wine vinegar is best)

STEP 1: Dump cabbage, olives, nuts, clams and raisins into large bowl.

STEP 2: In small bowl or cup, blend mayonnaise and vinegar together. Pour over slaw mixture. Season to taste and serve.

footnote: Use as a filling for pita bread, or eat right out of the bowl.

NEED:
- 1/2 small head RED CABBAGE
- 1/4 cup VEGETABLE OIL
- 1/2 cup SUGAR
- 1/4 cup CIDER VINEGAR
- dash GARLIC SALT, PEPPER
- to taste

STEP 1: Shred cabbage and dump in bowl.

STEP 2: In small saucepan, heat oil, sugar and vinegar on high heat. Stir and cook till dressing starts to boil. Remove from heat and pour over cabbage. Toss well to mix.

STEP 3: Season with garlic salt and pepper to your taste.

footnote: This salad tastes best when allowed to marinate in refrigerator overnight.

OR:

- **HOT SPINACH SALAD:**

While cabbage salad is still hot, toss with raw spinach (carefully washed, and patted dry on paper towels). Add 1 sliced hard-cooked egg, 1 tablespoon bacon bits and 2 thin-sliced green onions.

RED CABBAGE SALAD

10 MIN.

1 TO 2 SERVINGS

SOUPS & SALADS

BOWL & SMALL SAUCEPAN

TOP OF STOVE HIGH HEAT

SOMETHIN' DIFFERENT TUNA SALAD

5 MIN.

1 TO 2 SERVINGS

LARGE BOWL

NO COOKING

NEED:

1 6 oz. can TUNA, well drained
1 4 oz. can CHOPPED BLACK OLIVES
2 GREEN ONIONS, thinly sliced
2 HARD-COOKED EGGS, chopped
3/4 cup MAYONNAISE
1 teaspoon VINEGAR
SEASONED SALT
3 oz. CHOW MEIN NOODLES (optional)

Mix all together in bowl (except Chow Mein noodles). When ready to eat, top with Chow Mein noodles.

EXTRAS TO ADD:

- 1 stalk CELERY, chopped
- 1 CARROT, grated
- 1 2 oz. jar CHOPPED PIMIENTOS
- crumbled cooked BACON
- chopped RED APPLES
- spoonful sliced ALMONDS
- spoonful SUNFLOWER SEEDS
- handful BEAN SPROUTS
- spoonful RAISINS

footnote: Filling enough for a whole meal!

NEED:

    1 small bunch RAW SPINACH
    1/2 CUCUMBER, sliced thin
    1 11 oz. can MANDARIN ORANGES, drained
    bottled FRENCH DRESSING (or use Lemon & Oil Dressing, p. 26)
    6 MUSHROOMS, washed and sliced
    1 HARD-COOKED EGG, chopped

STEP 1: Wash spinach well and pat dry with paper towels. Tear spinach into bite-size pieces.

STEP 2: Dump spinach, cucumber and oranges into large salad bowl.

STEP 3: Add dressing (amount according to taste) and toss gently. Top with mushrooms and chopped egg.

footnote: Toss in sunflower seeds or peanuts for great taste.

SPINACH MANDARIN SALAD

5 MIN.

1 TO 2 SERVINGS

SOUPS & SALADS

SALAD BOWL

NO COOKING

HANDY HINT

Make too many pancakes?? Freeze the extras in a plastic bag with a sheet of waxed paper between layers. Remove from freezer number of pancakes needed and reheat in microwave on highest setting for 30 seconds.

To freshen stale crackers or chips, microwave between paper towels on HIGH for 30 seconds.

MICROWAVE MAGIC

NEED:
2 pieces uncooked CHICKEN, skin removed
1/2 cup bottled BARBECUE SAUCE
2 tablespoons BROWN SUGAR

STEP 1: Thoroughly wash chicken with water and pat dry with paper towels. Place chicken in microwave-safe shallow baking dish with meaty part of chicken to outer edge of dish.

STEP 2: Mix barbecue sauce with brown sugar. Spoon over chicken, turning chicken to coat both sides. Cover dish with plastic wrap and seal tightly.

STEP 3: Cook on HIGH 20 minutes, or till chicken pulls away from the bone easily and appears to be cooked through.

Tip: Whenever possible, remove the skin from chicken before cooking as skin has a high fat content and retains moisture, which can create "hot spots" in chicken and prevent equal cooking.

footnote: You can use as much sauce as you like during cooking; or pour it over chicken after cooked.

BARBECUED CHICKEN

20 MIN.

1 SERVING

MICROWAVE MAGIC

MICROWAVE-SAFE SHALLOW BAKING DISH

BROCCOLI ROLLS

5 MIN.

1 SERVING

**MICROWAVE-SAFE
SHALLOW BAKING
DISH**

NEED:
- 2 stalks FROZEN BROCCOLI
- 1 8 oz. jar PROCESSED CHEESE SPREAD, melted (see footnote)
- 2 slices COOKED HAM
- 2 slices TURKEY LUNCH MEAT

STEP 1: Rinse 2 stalks frozen broccoli in cold water to thaw, then pat dry with paper towel. Set aside.

STEP 2: Top ham slice with turkey slice. Repeat, then lay broccoli stalks on top with the flower part sticking out the ends. Roll up and place on microwave safe shallow baking dish. Pour melted cheese over.

STEP 3: Microwave on HIGH 3 minutes. (Rotate after 2 minutes if your microwave doesn't have a turntable.)

footnote: To melt cheese: remove lid on jar and microwave on HIGH 1 minute. (Use only the amount that appeals to you. Cover jar and keep rest of the cheese in refrigerator to be used later.)

NEED:
FLOUR TORTILLAS
CHEDDAR CHEESE, sliced or shredded
BUTTER or MARGARINE

OPTIONAL FILLINGS:
SALSA, BARBECUE SAUCE, thin sliced HAM, thin sliced COOKED
CHICKEN, mild CHILI PEPPERS, thin sliced ONIONS

STEP 1: Butter tortilla and lay on paper towel. Cover with cheese and top with whatever else appeals to you. Butter second tortilla and lay over fillings with butter side facing fillings.

STEP 2: Place quesadilla on paper towel and place in microwave. Microwave on HIGH 1½ to 2 minutes. Remove to plate and let cool a few minutes before cutting into triangles (pizza style).

EVERYONE'S FAVORITE QUESADILLAS

3 MIN.

1 SERVING

MICROWAVE MAGIC

PAPER TOWEL

LOW-CAL FISH & BROCCOLI

5 MIN.

1 SERVING

MICROWAVE MAGIC

MICROWAVE-SAFE SHALLOW BAKING DISH

NEED:
1 large piece uncooked chunky FISH
2 stalks FROZEN BROCCOLI
tablespoon BUTTER or MARGARINE
splash WHITE WINE
Optional:
sprinkle of DILL WEED, THYME or TARRAGON

STEP 1: Place fish in microwave-safe shallow baking dish. Top with broccoli stalks. Dot with butter. Sprinkle with herbs (if you have them). Spoon wine over all.

STEP 2: Cover tightly with plastic wrap. Cook on HIGH 5 minutes or till fish is flaky.

footnote: If you like it saucy, top with a couple spoonfuls of cheddar cheese soup (straight from the can). Do this during the final 2 minutes of cooking. This will add a few more calories but tastes great.

MICROWAVE MAGIC

MICROWAVE-SAFE COFFEE MUG

NEED:
- 1 cup MILK
- 1/4 teaspoon INSTANT COFFEE
- spoonful SUGAR or LOW-CAL SWEETENER

STEP 1: Fill cup with milk. Heat on HIGH 2 minutes or till milk is very hot.

STEP 2: Remove cup from microwave. Add coffee and stir well to mix completely. Add sugar if you like a sweet drink.

footnote: Very soothing. Use decaf coffee for a pleasant before-bedtime drink.

POTATOES, BAKED OR MASHED

4 MIN.

1 SERVING

MICROWAVE MAGIC

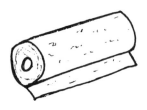

PAPER TOWEL

40

NEED:
> RUSSET or WHITE POTATOES
> VEGETABLE OIL

STEP 1: Wash and scrub potatoes to remove all dirt. Rub each potato with oil. Poke with fork in several places around potato.

STEP 2: Microwave on HIGH approximately 4 minutes per potato. Cooking time will vary depending on size, shape and density of potato.

STEP 3: When potato feels soft to the touch, remove and wrap in a paper towel or cloth and let sit 5 minutes. Potato will stay hot at least 30 minutes. Cut open and fill as you want.

- **QUICK MASHED POTATOES:**

Scoop out inside of well-cooked potato and mash with fork, adding 1 tablespoon butter and 1 tablespoon of milk to make it creamier. Salt and pepper to taste.

For a complete and filling meal, see ideas for potato stuffings on next page.

Top your BAKED POTATOES with any of the following for a filling meal:

CANNED CREAM-STYLE SOUP:
Pour into a large glass measuring cup or bowl. Stir and microwave on HIGH 3 to 6 minutes. Pour over potato. Top with green onions.

SHREDDED CHEDDAR CHEESE AND CRUMBLED COOKED BACON:
Lay 4 bacon strips on several sheets of paper towels and microwave on HIGH 4 minutes or till crisp. Crumble and sprinkle over cheese-topped potato. Microwave for 1/2 minute to melt cheese.

CHEATIN' CHILI, page 91

PEAS IN SNOW, page 113

MICROWAVE MAGIC

LARGE MICROWAVE-SAFE BOWL

SIMPLE SAUCES

4 MIN.

1 SERVING

LARGE MICROWAVE-SAFE BOWL

- **SOUPER SAUCE:**

Use can of condensed cream-style soup (not the ready-to-eat style). Empty soup into a microwave-safe bowl and heat on HIGH 3 minutes.
NOTE: NEVER put metal cans in microwave ovens (metal will spark and ignite under microwaves).

- **BASIC WHITE CREAM SAUCE:**

NEED:
>   2 tablespoons BUTTER or MARGARINE
>   2 tablespoons FLOUR
>   1 cup MILK
>   dash SALT

STEP 1: In large bowl, melt butter or margarine in microwave on HIGH 30 seconds.

STEP 2: Remove bowl from microwave and gradually stir in flour till well blended. Then stir in milk and salt. (Mixture may be slightly lumpy, but lumps disappear when cooked.) Heat on HIGH 2 minutes.

STEP 3: Remove, then give final stir. Cook on HIGH 2 more minutes or till smooth and creamy.

Use the directions for Basic White Cream Sauce (see preceding page)
Follow Step 1 and Step 2, then:

- **CHEESE SAUCE:**
Before you start Step 3, stir in 2 handfuls shredded cheddar cheese.
Continue with directions for Step 3.

- **BASIL-TOMATO SAUCE:**
Before you start Step 3, stir in 1 teaspoon tomato sauce and 1/4 teaspoon
dried basil (in spice section of market). Continue with directions for
Step 3.
Try over spinach pasta.

- **MUSTARD SAUCE:**
Before you start Step 3, stir in 1 teaspoon spicy mustard. Continue with
directions for Step 3.
Use with hot dogs as a dipping sauce.

- **LEMON SAUCE:**
Before you start Step 3, stir in 2 teaspoons lemon juice and 1 teaspoon
butter or margarine. Continue with Step 3.
Excellent over fish or vegetables.

SIMPLE SAUCES VARIATIONS

4 MIN.

1 SERVING

MICROWAVE MAGIC

LARGE MICROWAVE-SAFE BOWL

PERFECT SCRAMBLED EGGS

1 TO 1½ MIN.

1 SERVING

GLASS MEASURING CUP

NEED:
　　1 or 2 EGGS
　　SALT, PEPPER to taste

STEP 1: Crack egg(s) into a glass measuring cup. Beat well with a fork till all is yellow.

STEP 2: Cover cup tightly with plastic wrap.

STEP 3: Microwave at 70%, 1 minute for 1 egg (1½ minutes for 2 eggs). Should be perfect, but if you like your eggs done more, continue cooking at 70%, checking every 20 seconds.

Spoon out onto plate, add salt and pepper and eat.

footnote: NEVER microwave eggs in their shells; they will EXPLODE!!

10 MIN.

1 TO 2 SERVINGS

NEED:

    1 large ACORN SQUASH (it is the round dark-green one with ridges)
    scoop of COTTAGE CHEESE
    sprinkle WALNUTS, chopped
    1 tablespoon MARGARINE
    SALT, PEPPER to taste

STEP 1: Make about 6 small slits with a sharp knife around outside of squash. Only slit to inside center of squash; do not cut all the way through or cut open the squash.

STEP 2: Set in microwave. (No need for dish or paper towel under it.) Cook on HIGH 10 minutes.

NOTE: If you do not have a revolving base in your microwave, you will need to rotate the squash after the first 5 minutes, then continue cooking the remaining 5 minutes.

STEP 3: Remove the squash from microwave and let it sit about 5 to 10 minutes before cutting it open. (It is too hot to handle.) Then cut in half and remove seeds and pulp.

Fill squash with cottage cheese; top with walnuts. Add some butter and salt and pepper if you want.

MICROWAVE MAGIC

SHARP KNIFE

45

TORTILLA DOG

2 MIN.

1 SERVING

MICROWAVE MAGIC

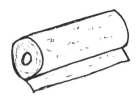

PAPER TOWEL

NEED:
large-size FLOUR TORTILLAS
HOT DOGS
BUTTER or MARGARINE

OPTIONAL CONDIMENTS:
BARBECUE SAUCE or CATSUP, CHILI, SHREDDED CHEESE,
MUSTARD, PICKLE RELISH

STEP 1: Butter tortilla and spread lightly with any condiment you like.

STEP 2: Lay hot dog on edge of tortilla and roll up. Wrap paper towel around tortilla dog.

STEP 3: Microwave on HIGH 1 to 2 minutes. Remove hot dog from microwave oven. Let hot dog remain wrapped up for one minute to cool before eating.

TEQUILA-SOAKED FISH

10 MIN.

1 TO 2 SERVINGS

NEED:
1/4 cup BUTTER or MARGARINE
handful SLICED ALMONDS
juice of 1 LEMON
sprinkle of DILL WEED (in spice section of market)
SALT, PEPPER to taste
1 tablespoon TEQUILA
1 or 2 pieces white CHUNKY FISH (bass, halibut, turbot, etc.)

STEP 1: Put butter and almonds in microwave-safe shallow baking dish. Cook on HIGH 3 minutes, stir, then continue on HIGH 2 more minutes or till almonds are golden. Remove from microwave oven.

STEP 2: Stir in rest of ingredients, laying fish on top. Spoon some of the sauce over fish.

STEP 3: Cover with plastic wrap. Cook on HIGH 5 minutes or till fish is flaky. (Don't overcook or fish will be tough.)

footnote: Serve this with packaged rice mix and spoon sauce over.

MICROWAVE-SAFE SHALLOW BAKING DISH

47

HANDY HINT

For fresh parsley and alfalfa sprouts, try growing your own in small pots
by a sunny window.

To remove onion odor from your hands, rub them with celery.

VEGETARIAN MAIN MEALS

15-MINUTE MACARONI AND CHEESE

1 TO 2 SERVINGS

VEGETARIAN MAIN MEALS

LARGE SAUCEPAN TOP OF STOVE

MEDIUM HEAT

NEED:
8 oz. MACARONI
1 cup AMERICAN CHEESE, cut in cubes, or
1/2 cup PROCESSED CHEESE SPREAD
SALT, PEPPER to taste

STEP 1: In large saucepan, cook macaroni according to directions on package. Drain well. Remove from heat.

STEP 2: Add cheese to HOT macaroni, stirring till melted. Season to taste. Serve.

footnote: Fast and nutritious. Tastes great with a gelatin salad.

BASIC STIR-FRY SAUCE

2 MIN.

1 SERVING

SMALL BOWL

HIGH HEAT

NEED:

1/2 teaspoon INSTANT CHICKEN BOUILLON
1/4 cup HOT WATER
splash SOY SAUCE
1 teaspoon CORNSTARCH

STEP 1: In small cup or bowl, dissolve bouillon in hot water.

STEP 2: Add rest of ingredients. Stir.

STEP 3: Pour over hot stir-fried vegetables. Cook and stir on high heat 1 minute or till sauce thickens.

• CORNSTARCH is in the baking section of the market, and INSTANT BOUILLON is in the soup section of the market.

footnote: If you like a thicker sauce, add more cornstarch.

NEED:
  couple handfuls fresh or frozen VEGETABLES, cut into bite-size pieces
  2 tablespoons VEGETABLE OIL
  splash SOY SAUCE
  splash SHERRY (optional)

STEP 1: In skillet, heat oil on high heat till very hot. Stir in vegetables. (There will be a lot of noise and spattering.)

STEP 2: Stir quickly (approximately 5 minutes) on high heat till vegetables are tender but still bright in color.

STEP 3: Add a splash of soy sauce and sherry (if you have some). Stir and serve.

footnote: In place of Step 3, try Stir-Fry Sauce on previous page.

SKILLET TOP OF STOVE

HIGH HEAT

HOT TACO SALAD

15 MIN.

1 TO 2 SERVINGS

SKILLET
TOP OF STOVE

MEDIUM LOW HEAT

NEED:
1 8 oz. can REFRIED BEANS (check for a brand made without lard)
6-8 CHERRY TOMATOES, cut in half
1/4 HEAD LETTUCE, shredded
handful shredded CHEDDAR CHEESE
couple handfuls TORTILLA CHIPS (or corn chips)

STEP 1: Heat beans in skillet on medium low heat till very hot.

STEP 2: Turn off heat. Add the rest of the ingredients. Stir gently.

STEP 3: Sprinkle more grated cheese on top and, if you need to save time and dishwashing, eat right out of the pan.

NEED:

- 1 small ONION, finely chopped
- 1 clove GARLIC, mashed
- 1 tablespoon VEGETABLE OIL
- 1 16 oz. can WHOLE ITALIAN TOMATOES, cut up
- 1 15½ oz. can TOMATO SAUCE
- 1 6 oz. can TOMATO PASTE (use less for thinner sauce)
- splash RED WINE
- 1 tablespoon ITALIAN HERB SEASONING
- 1 tablespoon SALT

STEP 1: In saucepan, on medium high heat, cook onion and garlic in hot oil till lightly browned.

STEP 2: Stir in rest of ingredients. When sauce comes to a boil, reduce heat to lowest setting. Cover tightly and cook minimum of 30 minutes (longer cooking enhances flavor).

STEP 3: Remove lid and cook 15 more minutes. Serve over hot pasta.

footnote: Freezes well.

MEATLESS SPAGHETTI SAUCE

45 MIN.

3 TO 4 SERVINGS

VEGETARIAN MAIN MEALS

SAUCEPAN WITH LID
TOP OF STOVE

MEDIUM HIGH TO
LOWEST HEAT

PASTA WITH PESTO SAUCE

5 MIN.

1 TO 2 SERVINGS

VEGETARIAN MAIN MEALS

SMALL BOWL

NO COOKING

NEED:
1/2 cup fresh PARSLEY, chopped fine and packed in cup
1 tablespoon DRIED BASIL
1/2 teaspoon SALT
dash PEPPER
4 CLOVES GARLIC (remove outer skin and crush well)
1/3 cup OLIVE OIL
1 tablespoon MARGARINE
1 tablespoon BOILING WATER
1/2 cup grated PARMESAN CHEESE
1/4 cup PINE NUTS (or walnuts), finely chopped

1/2 lb. hot cooked PASTA

STEP 1: In small bowl, combine all ingredients except pasta.

STEP 2: Stir well with fork to blend flavors.

STEP 3: Pour sauce (it will be thick) over hot pasta and toss well to coat thoroughly.

FANTASTIC!!

NEED:

    1 cup MILK
    1/2 cup PACKAGED PANCAKE MIX (e.g., Bisquick)
    2 EGGS
    2 tablespoons BUTTER or MARGARINE
    3/4 cup grated JACK, WHITE, CHEDDAR or SWISS CHEESE
    1/2 cup FROZEN CUT-UP BROCCOLI

Preheat oven to 350°

STEP 1: Combine all ingredients, except broccoli, in blender container. Blend on low speed 1 minute.

STEP 2: Thaw broccoli in cold water, drain and pat dry with paper towel.

STEP 3: Spread a bit of butter around inside of pie pan. Lay broccoli in bottom of pie pan. Pour blender mixture over broccoli (being careful not to spill over sides). Bake in 350° oven 40 minutes or till quiche is puffy and golden and doesn't jiggle when you move it.

footnote: You might want to try this with spinach for a terrific spinach quiche!!

QUICHE IN A BLENDER

45 MIN.

3 TO 4 SERVINGS

VEGETARIAN MAIN MEALS

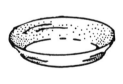

BLENDER &
8" PIE PAN

350° OVEN

SURPRISE "MEAT" LOAF

1½ HOURS

3 TO 4 SERVINGS

2 QT. LOAF PAN

350° OVEN

NEED:
- 2 cups BREAD CRUMBS (see footnote)
- 1 cup WALNUTS, finely ground (see footnote)
- 1/2 cup MILK
- 2 EGGS
- 1 teaspoon GARLIC SALT
- 1 teaspoon DRIED PARSLEY
- 1 teaspoon SAGE (in spice section of market)

Preheat oven to 350°

STEP 1: Thoroughly mix all ingredients together in a large mixing bowl.

STEP 2: Grease loaf-shaped baking dish generously with margarine. Pour mixture into dish.

STEP 3: Bake in 350° oven approximately 1½ hours or till knife inserted into loaf comes out dry. Remove from oven and let cool till you can remove easily onto plate. Tastes great hot or cold in sandwiches.

footnote: Use your blender to make quick bread crumbs. Simply tear a slice of bread into quarters and blend on medium speed till crumbly. Best to do 1 slice at a time. You will need 3 to 4 slices bread for 2 cups crumbs.

Need finely ground nuts? Use your blender again.

NEED:

- 3 tablespoons VEGETABLE OIL (or better yet, OLIVE OIL)
- 1 ZUCCHINI, thinly sliced
- 2 CARROTS, thinly sliced
- 1/2 each RED and GREEN BELL PEPPER, chopped into bite-size pieces
- 1 ONION, thinly sliced
- (any other fresh veg you want, sliced thin)
- 1/2 small head RED CABBAGE (important ingredient)
- 1 tablespoon WINE VINEGAR
- SALT, PEPPER to taste

STEP 1: In large skillet, on high heat, heat oil till hot (drop of water will sizzle in pan). Carefully add all vegetables except cabbage. Stir and fry about 5 minutes or till veg are bright in color and still crispy.

STEP 2: Add cabbage, vinegar, salt and pepper. Stir and fry on medium heat 10 minutes or till all ingredients are hot and cabbage becomes tender and slightly limp.

footnote: Tastes wonderful with buttered pasta.

VEGETABLE SUPREME

15 MIN.

1 TO 2 SERVINGS

VEGETARIAN MAIN MEALS

SKILLET
TOP OF STOVE

HIGH TO MEDIUM HEAT

WESTERN BURRITOS

10 MIN.

1 SERVING

VEGETARIAN MAIN MEALS

SKILLET
TOP OF STOVE

MEDIUM HEAT

NEED:
2 EGGS, lightly beaten with fork
1 tablespoon MARGARINE
spoonful grated CHEDDAR CHEESE
1/2 ONION, finely chopped
spoonful BARBECUE SAUCE
large FLOUR TORTILLA

STEP 1: In skillet, on medium heat, melt margarine. Cook and stir eggs till almost done to your liking. Add cheese and onion. Gently stir and cook 1 minute. Remove to plate.

STEP 2: Quickly heat tortilla on dry hot skillet. (Watch, don't burn.)

STEP 3: Spread egg mixture on tortilla. Spoon barbecue sauce over and fold up, burrito style.

NEED:

2 tablespoons VEGETABLE OIL
1/2 small ONION, thinly sliced
1 small RED POTATO, thinly sliced
1 ZUCCHINI, thinly sliced
splash SOY SAUCE
sprinkle PARMESAN CHEESE
4 EGGS, lightly beaten with fork

STEP 1: In skillet, on high heat, cook onions and potato in hot oil till onion is transparent (approximately 2 minutes).

STEP 2: Add zucchini, soy sauce and Parmesan cheese. Reduce heat to medium low. Cook 5 minutes, stirring occasionally.

STEP 3: Pour eggs over vegetables. Cover and cook on low heat 5 minutes. Eggs will puff like an omelet.

ZUCCHINI & EGGS FRITTATA

15 MIN.

1 TO 2 SERVINGS

VEGETARIAN MAIN MEALS

SKILLET WITH LID TOP OF STOVE

HIGH TO LOW HEAT

HANDY HINT

Rub chicken with lemon when washing. Flavors and cleans at the same time.

Safety tip: Always wash counter surface with hot soapy water and rinse well both before and after cleaning poultry. This helps to prevent salmonella bacteria from forming or being transferred to other foods.

CHICKEN

NEED:

    1 FRYING CHICKEN, cut up
    1 can CREAM OF CHICKEN or CREAM OF MUSHROOM SOUP
    1 4 oz. can MUSHROOMS, drained
    1/2 cup SHERRY or DRY WHITE WINE
    PAPRIKA (in spice section of market)

Preheat oven to 325°

STEP 1: Wash chicken and pat dry with paper towels. Place in baking dish.

STEP 2: In small bowl, blend together soup, mushrooms and wine.

STEP 3: Pour over chicken. Sprinkle with paprika. Bake in 325° oven 1½ hours, or till chicken is tender.

Looks Fancy! Tastes Delicious!

CHICKEN IN WINE

1½ HOURS

3 TO 4 SERVINGS

CHICKEN

OVEN-PROOF BAKING DISH

325° OVEN

CHICKEN ON A DIET

1 HOUR

3 TO 4 SERVINGS

CHICKEN

FOIL-LINED BROILER PAN

325° OVEN

NEED:
1 FRYING CHICKEN, cut up
SALT, PEPPER to taste
1 can DIET ORANGE SODA
1/4 cup SOY SAUCE

Preheat oven to 325°

STEP 1: Wash chicken (remove skin) and pat dry with paper towels. Salt and pepper chicken and place in foil-lined broiler pan.

STEP 2: Mix together orange soda and soy sauce. Pour over chicken.

STEP 3: Bake in 325° oven 1 hour or till chicken is tender. Spoon sauce over chicken couple of times while cooking.

footnote: Great to nibble on next day.

NEED:
3-4 CHICKEN PARTS
1/4 cup HONEY
2 teaspoons MUSTARD
2 tablespoons SOY SAUCE
1/2 teaspoon CURRY POWDER (spice section of market)

Preheat oven to 350°

STEP 1: Mix together in pie pan to make sauce: honey, mustard, soy sauce, curry powder.

STEP 2: Wash chicken and pat dry with paper toweling. Dip chicken in sauce to coat well. Place on foil-lined broiler pan.

STEP 3: Bake uncovered in 350° oven 30 minutes. Turn chicken pieces over and bake 20-30 more minutes or till chicken is tender.

footnote: Stick a potato in oven to bake as chicken cooks.

CURRIED CHICKEN

50 MIN.

1 TO 2 SERVINGS

CHICKEN

PIE PAN & FOIL-LINED BROILER PAN

350° OVEN

GIZZARDS IN GRAVY

60 MIN.

SEVERAL SERVINGS

CHICKEN

SAUCEPAN WITH LID TOP OF STOVE

HIGH TO LOW HEAT

NEED:
1 pkg. uncooked CHICKEN GIZZARDS
2 cups WATER
1/2 ONION, chopped
1/2 teaspoon INSTANT CHICKEN BOUILLON
SALT, PEPPER to taste
1/3 cup FLOUR
1/4 cup WATER

STEP 1: Wash chicken and place in saucepan. Add 2 cups water, onion, bouillon, dash each salt and pepper. Bring to boil on high heat.

STEP 2: Reduce heat to very low. Cover and cook slowly 1 hour.

STEP 3: In separate cup, stir flour into water till smooth. Slowly pour into chicken and broth, stirring constantly. Turn heat up to medium. Cook and stir 2 minutes.

footnote: Serve over hot rice or noodles.

NEED:

3-4 CHICKEN PIECES
1/2 cup bottled BARBECUE SAUCE
2 tablespoons MARGARINE, melted
large tablespoon BROWN SUGAR
SALT, PEPPER

Preheat oven to 350˚

STEP 1: Wash chicken and pat dry with paper towels. In small bowl, stir together barbecue sauce, margarine and brown sugar.

STEP 2: Lay chicken in foil-lined broiler pan. Season with salt and pepper. Brush half of sauce mixture on chicken and bake uncovered in 350˚ oven 30 minutes.

STEP 3: Turn chicken pieces over and brush with rest of sauce. Cook till tender, 20 or 30 more minutes.

footnote: If too much liquid in pan, spoon out some.

OVEN-BARBECUED CHICKEN

1 HOUR

1 TO 2 SERVINGS

CHICKEN

FOIL-LINED BROILER PAN

350˚ OVEN

OVEN-BAKED CHICKEN

1 HOUR

1 TO 2 SERVINGS

CHICKEN

FOIL-LINED BROILER PAN

350° OVEN

NEED:

3-4 CHICKEN PIECES
2 tablespoons MARGARINE
SALT, PEPPER, PAPRIKA, GARLIC SALT

Preheat oven to 350°

STEP 1: Wash chicken and pat dry with paper towels.

STEP 2: Melt margarine in foil-lined broiler pan. Lay chicken in pan and turn to coat with margarine. Season lightly.

STEP 3: Bake uncovered in 350° oven 30 minutes. Turn chicken pieces over and season. Continue cooking 20 more minutes or till golden and tender.

NEED:
4 DRUMSTICKS or 2 whole CHICKEN LEGS
2 tablespoons MAYONNAISE
1 cup crushed CORN CHIPS
1 teaspoon CHILI POWDER
dash SALT
teaspoon MARGARINE

Preheat oven to 375°

STEP 1: Wash chicken and pat dry with paper towels. Spread mayonnaise on chicken.

STEP 2: In small bowl, combine corn chips, chili powder and salt. Stir well. Roll chicken in mixture.

STEP 3: Generously grease pan with margarine. Lay chicken in pan. Bake in 375° oven 40 minutes or till chicken is browned and tender.

SPICY LEGS

30 MIN.

1 TO 2 SERVINGS

CHICKEN

SHALLOW BAKING DISH

375° OVEN

OTHER CHICKEN RECIPES FOUND IN THIS COOKBOOK

COOKED CHICKEN:

MICROWAVE:

HANDY HINT

When a recipe calls for bread crumbs, try using ready-to-eat flaked cereal instead.

FISH

BAKED FISH IN SOUR CREAM

30 MIN.

1 TO 2 SERVINGS

SHALLOW BAKING DISH

350° OVEN

NEED:
FISH FILLETS
2 tablespoons MARGARINE
SALT, PEPPER, PAPRIKA
2 teaspoons MAYONNAISE
4 teaspoons SOUR CREAM
1 4 oz. can MUSHROOMS, drained, or 6 FRESH MUSHROOMS, sliced

Preheat oven to 350°

STEP 1: Grease shallow baking dish with dab of margarine. Lay fish in dish. Dot fish with margarine and lightly season.

STEP 2: In a small bowl, mix mayonnaise and sour cream. Cover fish with mixture. Top with mushrooms.

STEP 3: Bake in 350° oven 30 minutes or till fish is flaky.

CHEESY FISHSTICKS & BROCCOLI

20 MIN.

2 TO 3 SERVINGS

FISH

**SAUCEPAN
WITH LID
TOP OF STOVE**

**FOIL-LINED
BROILER
PAN**

**MEDIUM HEAT
425° OVEN**

NEED:
1 small pkg. FROZEN FISH STICKS
1 10 oz. pkg. FROZEN CHOPPED BROCCOLI
1 can CHEDDAR CHEESE SOUP
2 tablespoons MILK
dash SEASONED SALT
LEMON

Preheat oven to 425°

STEP 1: Lay fish in bottom of foil-lined broiler pan. Bake in 425° oven 10 minutes.

STEP 2: While fish bakes, cook broccoli according to directions on package. Drain.

STEP 3: Gently stir into cooked broccoli: soup, milk and seasoned salt. Cook on low heat. Spoon over baked fish in broiler pan. Return to oven for 5 minutes.

Squeeze lemon over and serve.

NEED:

2 uncooked RED POTATOES, thinly sliced
6⅛ oz. can TUNA, drained
5 oz. can WATER CHESTNUTS (store the rest in refrigerator and use in salads later)
1 stalk CELERY
1 can CHEDDAR CHEESE SOUP
1/3 soup can MILK
1 8½ oz. can GREEN BEANS, drained
handful PEANUTS or FRIED CHOW MEIN NOODLES

Preheat oven to 350°

STEP 1: Lay potato slices in bottom of shallow baking dish. Top with tuna, water chestnuts, and celery.

STEP 2: In small bowl, stir together soup and milk. Pour half of mixture over casserole. Top with green beans; then pour remaining sauce over all.

STEP 3: Bake in 350° oven 40 minutes or till potatoes are tender when you poke them with a fork. Sprinkle with nuts or chow mein noodles and serve.

CHINESE TUNA CASSEROLE

40 MIN.

1 TO 2 SERVINGS

FISH

SHALLOW BAKING DISH

350° OVEN

FISH TACOS

10 MIN.

1 SERVING

SKILLET
TOP OF STOVE

HIGH HEAT

NEED:
    2 FROZEN FISH STICKS, the chunky kind
    4 CORN TORTILLAS (soft uncooked)
    handful shredded CABBAGE
    1/2 TOMATO, chopped
    spoonful bottled TARTAR SAUCE
    sprinkle shredded CHEDDAR CHEESE
    large spoonful SALSA

STEP 1: Cook fish according to directions on package.

STEP 2: Heat skillet on high heat 1 minute. Lay tortilla in skillet and heat on one side for a few seconds; turn over and heat other side. When tortilla is hot and limp, remove and continue with second tortilla.

STEP 3: Place two hot tortillas together and lay hot cooked fish in center. Sprinkle with cabbage, cheese, tomato, tartar sauce and salsa. Fold in half and eat "taco style."

footnote: Recipe makes two tacos. If you want more, make sure you use two tortillas for each fish taco.

NEED:

1 FISH FILLET
SALT, PEPPER, PAPRIKA to taste
juice of 1/2 LEMON
1 teaspoon PARSLEY, chopped
2 tablespoons WHITE WINE
1 tablespoon MARGARINE

Preheat oven to 350°

STEP 1: Lay fish in shallow baking dish.

STEP 2: Sprinkle fish with seasonings, lemon juice and parsley. Pour wine over.

STEP 3: Dot fish with margarine. Bake in 350° oven, 20 minutes or till fish is flaky.

footnote: Pour sauce in pan over cooked fish.

FRESH FISH IN WHITE WINE

20 MIN.

1 TO 2 SERVINGS

FISH

SHALLOW BAKING DISH

350° OVEN

GOOD OLE MACARONI-TUNA CASSEROLE

20 MIN.

1 TO 2 SERVINGS

FISH

OVENPROOF PAN OR SKILLET

350° OVEN

NEED:

1 box MACARONI AND CHEESE dinner mix
1 6⅛ oz. can TUNA, drained
1 can CREAM OF CELERY SOUP
1/2 cup MILK
handful grated CHEDDAR CHEESE

Preheat oven to 350°

STEP 1: Cook macaroni according to directions on box, using ovenproof saucepan or skillet.

STEP 2: Add tuna, soup and milk to cooked macaroni and cheese. Stir well.

STEP 3: Sprinkle cheese on top and bake in 350° oven till cheese is bubbly (approximately 15 minutes).

footnote: Add any leftover cooked vegetables you have to Step 2.

NEED:
1 HALIBUT STEAK
1 LEMON
1 small TOMATO, chopped
1 CARROT, grated
1 GREEN ONION, sliced

Preheat oven to 350°

STEP 1: Place halibut in shallow baking dish. Squeeze lemon over fish.

STEP 2: Mix vegetables together in small bowl and spread over halibut.

STEP 3: Cover dish with foil and bake in 350° oven 20 minutes.

JUST FOR THE HALIBUT

20 MIN.

1 TO 2 SERVINGS

FISH

SHALLOW BAKING DISH

350° OVEN

TUNA SOUFFLÉ

45 MIN.

1 TO 2 SERVINGS

FISH

SHALLOW BAKING DISH

350° OVEN

NEED:
- 4 slices BREAD (good way to use up stale bread)
- 4 slices CHEESE
- 6⅛ oz. can TUNA, drained
- 3 EGGS, beaten with fork till fluffy and yellow
- 1 cup MILK
- 1 GREEN ONION, sliced
- 1 2 oz. can SLICED MUSHROOMS
- dash SALT, PEPPER

STEP 1: Grease bottom and sides of baking dish with dab of margarine or vegetable oil. Lay 2 bread slices over bottom of baking dish. Top with cheese, tuna and remaining 2 bread slices.

STEP 2: In small bowl, stir together eggs, milk, onion, mushrooms, salt and pepper. Pour over layered mixture in baking dish. Set dish to the side for 15 minutes while you preheat oven to 350°.

STEP 3: Bake in 350° oven 45 minutes. Serve hot and puffy.

HANDY HINT

 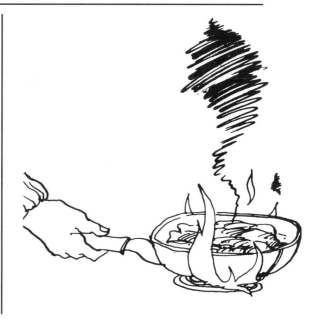

Drain cooked meat fat into old can & discard when solidified.
DON'T DUMP IT DOWN THE DRAIN!

Don't ruin fresh fish by using too high a temperature and overcooking.

Don't leave perishable foods out of refrigerator. They *will spoil!* To thaw frozen steaks, thaw in vegetable oil. Density of oil holds in juices.

MEATY MEALS

NEED:

  1 large KNOCKWURST or BALONEY
  1 tablespoon MARGARINE
  1/4 RED ONION, chopped
  1 8 oz. can SAUERKRAUT
  couple spoonfuls SOUR CREAM

STEP 1: In skillet, on medium heat, cook onion in margarine 1 minute or till onion is transparent.

STEP 2: Place meat in skillet and add sauerkraut. Cover and heat till hot.

STEP 3: Remove from heat and stir in sour cream till just hot. Serve.

BALONEY & KRAUT

15 MIN.

1 SERVING

SKILLET WITH LID TOP OF STOVE

MEDIUM HEAT

BEST BEEF STEW

4 HOURS

2-3 SERVINGS

OVENPROOF PAN WITH LID

300° OVEN (OR SLOW COOKER)

NEED:
- 1 lb. lean STEWING BEEF
- 2 CARROTS, cut in chunks
- 2 ONIONS, cut in chunks
- 1 POTATO, cut in chunks
- 1 stalk CELERY, cut in chunks
- 1 15 oz. can cut-up TOMATOES, undrained
- 1/4 cup MINUTE TAPIOCA (important ingredient)
- dash of THYME and OREGANO
- 1/2 teaspoon SALT
- 1 heaping teaspoon INSTANT COFFEE
- 1 BEEF BOUILLON CUBE (or 1 teaspoon instant bouillon)
- 2 cups WATER

STEP 1: Dump all ingredients into a large ovenproof pan. Stir to mix well and cover.

STEP 2: Cook in 300° oven 4 hours or till meat is tender. (If you get the chance, stir a couple of times during cooking.)

footnote: If you use a slow cooker, you'll love the aroma when you come home starving after classes all day.

NEED:

    2 tablespoons VEGETABLE OIL
    couple spoonfuls FLOUR
    1 lb. STEWING BEEF, cut in bite-size pieces
    1 ONION, chopped
    1 can condensed CREAM OF MUSHROOM SOUP
    1 5 oz. can TOMATO SAUCE
    couple pinches TARRAGON, optional (in spice section of market)
    1 cup BURGUNDY or any cheap red wine

STEP 1: Put flour in plastic bag. Add meat and shake to cover all pieces.

STEP 2: In large saucepan, heat oil on high heat. Add floured beef, then onion. Stir and cook till meat is browned on all sides.

STEP 3: Stir in soup, tomato sauce, tarragon and wine. Bring sauce to a boil, then turn heat down to lowest setting. Cook slowly 2 to 3 hours, or till beef is tender. (Check a couple of times during cooking to make sure nothing is sticking. If you find that it is sticking, add about 1/2 cup water and continue cooking.)

This is a great dish for a crock pot or slow cooker (if you have one).

footnote: Excellent served over rice with a plop of sour cream on top.

BEEF BURGUNDY

3 HRS.

2 TO 3 SERVINGS

MEATY MEALS

LARGE HEAVY SAUCEPAN WITH LID TOP OF STOVE

HIGH TO LOW HEAT

BEEF MEXICANA

15 MIN.

1 TO 2 SERVINGS

**SKILLET WITH LID
TOP OF STOVE**

**MEDIUM TO LOWEST
HEAT**

NEED:
1 ONION, sliced thin
1 clove GARLIC, mashed
1 tablespoon MARGARINE
1/2 lb. GROUND BEEF
1 8 oz. can TOMATO SAUCE
1 8 oz. can WHOLE KERNEL CORN
splash HOT TACO SAUCE
SALT, PEPPER to taste

STEP 1: In skillet, on medium heat, cook onion and garlic in margarine till golden.

STEP 2: Add ground beef. Stir and cook till beef loses pink color.

STEP 3: Stir in tomato sauce, corn, taco sauce and seasonings. Reduce heat to lowest heat. Cover and cook 10 minutes.

footnote: Crunch up tortilla chips and sprinkle on top just before eating.

NEED:

1 tablespoon VEGETABLE OIL
1/2 lb. GROUND BEEF
1 ONION, chopped
1 clove GARLIC, minced
1/4 GREEN BELL PEPPER, chopped
1 can (15 oz.) CHILI
1 can (15 oz.) KIDNEY BEANS
1 15 oz. can CRUSHED TOMATOES (don't use stewed tomatoes)
1 oz. jar SALSA (mild or hot, as you like it)
1/2 cup cheap RED WINE
SALT, PEPPER

STEP 1: Heat oil in large saucepan on high heat. Add ground beef, onion and garlic. Stir and cook till meat is crumbly and browned. (Drain off excess grease into an old can to discard later.)

STEP 2: Add rest of ingredients and stir well. When chili starts to boil turn heat to lowest setting. Cover pan and cook slowly for at least 1/2 hour. Be sure to stir a couple of times during cooking.

footnote: If you have the time, 4 to 5 hours' cooking allows flavors to blend for an even better taste.

CHEATIN' CHILI

45 MIN TO 4 HRS.

2 TO 3 SERVINGS

MEATY MEALS

LARGE SAUCEPAN WITH LID TOP OF STOVE

LOW HEAT

CHEAP ROAST

3 HOURS

2 TO 3 SERVINGS

HEAVY-DUTY ALUMINUM FOIL

350° OVEN

NEED:
   "Cheap" ROUND BONE or BLADE-CUT ROAST
   1 pkg. DRY ONION SOUP MIX
   1 can condensed CREAM OF MUSHROOM SOUP
   ALUMINUM FOIL, wide heavy-duty

Preheat oven to 350°

STEP 1: Tear off about 2½–3 feet of foil. Fold in half.

STEP 2: Lay roast in middle of foil. Spread both soups over roast. Wrap and seal so juices won't drip out.

STEP 3: Cook in 350° oven 3 hours. Be careful when you unwrap foil, so juices won't spill.

No cleanup!

footnote: Makes its own gravy. Serve with mashed potatoes and hot vegetable.

NEED:

    1 lb. GROUND BEEF
    2/3 cup packaged BREAD STUFFING MIX
    2 teaspoons dry MINCED ONIONS (in spice section of market)
    1 EGG
    3/4 cup WATER
    1 teaspoon SALT
    dash PEPPER

Preheat oven to 350°

STEP 1: Dump all ingredients into large bowl; mix well. Shape into small balls (approximately 1½").

STEP 2: Place on a cookie sheet and bake in 350° oven 15 minutes or till browned.

footnote: Use in spaghetti sauce, soups and with gravies. Or slice and use in sandwiches. Freeze extra meatballs in plastic bag.

FAST & EASY MEATBALLS

15 MIN.

15–20 MEATBALLS

MEATY MEALS

COOKIE SHEET OR BROILER PAN (NO RACK)

350° OVEN

GREG'S HAWAIIAN TERIYAKI SAUCE

5 MIN.

AS MUCH AS YOU NEED

SAUCEPAN TOP OF STOVE

MEDIUM HEAT

94

NEED:
- 1/2 cup SOY SAUCE
- 1/2 cup SUGAR
- 1 clove GARLIC
- 1/2 teaspoon GROUND GINGER (in spice section of market)

STEP 1: In saucepan, on medium heat, combine soy sauce and sugar. Stir and heat till sugar is dissolved.

STEP 2: Mash garlic clove with bottom of flat glass. Add garlic and ginger to sauce. Bring sauce to a boil. Remove from heat and let stand till just warm.

Use to marinate (soak) meat 10 minutes before cooking; or brush on meat during cooking.

footnote: Makes tough meat tender. Use on steak, chicken or hamburgers.

NEED:

- 1 tablespoon VEGETABLE OIL
- 1/2 lb. GROUND BEEF
- 1 POTATO, cut in bite-size pieces
- 1/2 ONION, sliced thin
- 1 10 oz. can BEEF GRAVY
- couple pinches PARSLEY (fresh, if available)
- pinch of THYME (optional)
- SALT, PEPPER to taste

STEP 1: In skillet, on medium heat, heat oil till hot. Add ground beef. Stir and cook till brown and crumbly. (Drain off excess fat into an old can.)

STEP 2: Add remaining ingredients; stir to mix.

STEP 3: Cover and cook on lowest heat 20 minutes, stirring occasionally.

footnote: In place of potato, use cooked noodles and reduce time in Step 3 to 10 minutes.

HAMBURGER HASH

25 MIN.

1 TO 2 SERVINGS

MEATY MEALS

SKILLET WITH LID
TOP OF STOVE

MEDIUM HEAT

HASH PATTIES

10 MIN.

1 TO 2 SERVINGS

**SKILLET
TOP OF STOVE**

HIGH HEAT

NEED:
1 tablespoon VEGETABLE OIL
1 1 lb. can CORNED BEEF HASH
1/2 ONION, chopped
1/4 GREEN BELL PEPPER, chopped
plop CATSUP
large spoonful PICKLE RELISH
dash PEPPER

STEP 1: In large mixing bowl, dump together all ingredients and mix well. Shape into 4 small patties.

STEP 2: Heat oil in large skillet on high heat. Gently lay in patties. Cook till brown on underside and try to turn over. (They will probably fall apart, but keep at it till all the hash is turned over and browned on both sides.)

footnote: This may look messy, but it tastes delicious. Have with potatoes and veg.

FIRST: Make Mom's Mashed Potatoes (see recipe, p. 112) and set aside.

NEED:
4 MILD ITALIAN SAUSAGES
1/2 GREEN BELL PEPPER, cut in strips
1/2 ONION, cut in strips
couple plops bottled STEAK SAUCE (e.g., Heinz 57, A-1, or HP Sauce)

STEP 1: Pierce each sausage with a fork a couple of times. Lay sausages in skillet and just barely cover with water. Turn heat to high. When water starts to boil, turn heat to medium and gently cook 25 minutes. (Check to make sure water doesn't boil out.) Drain any excess water out of pan.

STEP 2: Add vegetables and steak sauce to pan with sausages and cook on medium 5 to 10 minutes or till vegetables are done to your liking. (You can add more sauce if you like.)

footnote: Serve sausage hot over mashed potatoes. Add a crisp green salad.

ITALIAN SAUSAGE & MASH

30 MIN.

1 TO 2 SERVINGS

MEATY MEALS

SKILLET
TOP OF STOVE

MEDIUM HEAT

MEAT LOAF EVERYONE LIKES

45 MIN.

2 TO 3 SERVINGS

BAKING DISH

340° OVEN

NEED:
> 1 EGG
> 1/4 cup MILK
> 2 slices SOFT BREAD, crumbled up
> 1 lb. GROUND BEEF
> 1 4 oz. can MUSHROOMS (stems and pieces)
> couple plops CATSUP
> 1/2 pkg. DRY ONION SOUP MIX (shake well before using)

Preheat oven to 350°

STEP 1: In large bowl, beat egg with fork. Add milk and bread crumbs. Stir to mix.

STEP 2: Dump in rest of the ingredients and stir to mix well.

STEP 3: Dump mixture into oven baking dish and mold into a loaf. Bake in 350° oven 45 minutes or till done to your liking.

footnote: Makes great cold sandwiches next day.

NEED:

3-4 PORK CHOPS
1 tablespoon MARGARINE
6 oz. can FROZEN ORANGE JUICE
1 spoonful BROWN SUGAR
splash WHITE WINE (or SHERRY or WATER)
pinch of GROUND GINGER (optional)

STEP 1: In skillet, on medium heat, fry pork chops in margarine till light brown on each side.

STEP 2: Combine all other ingredients in a bowl. Pour over pork in skillet.

STEP 3: Cover and reduce heat to lowest setting. Cook 35-45 minutes.

Serve over rice.

footnote: Cook pork till there is no pink coloring in the meat when you cut through it.

PORK CHOPS A L'ORANGE

45 MIN.

1 TO 2 SERVINGS

MEATY MEALS

SKILLET WITH LID TOP OF STOVE

MEDIUM TO LOWEST HEAT

SPAM & EGGS

5 MIN.

1 TO 2 SERVINGS

**SKILLET
TOP OF STOVE**

MEDIUM HIGH HEAT

100

NEED:
> 7 oz. can SPAM, cut in thin strips
> 1 tablespoon MARGARINE
> 3 EGGS, lightly beaten with fork
> 1 8 oz. can CREAM-STYLE CORN
> 1 GREEN ONION, thinly sliced

STEP 1: In skillet, on medium high heat, quickly brown meat in margarine.

STEP 2: Combine eggs, corn and green onion. Pour over meat.

STEP 3: Cook, stirring occasionally till eggs are soft scrambled.

footnote: Use cooked leftover ham in place of spam.

NEED:

1 tablespoon VEGETABLE OIL
4–5 WAFER-THIN PORK CHOPS
1 small ONION, sliced
1 can CREAM OF CHICKEN soup
1 plop CATSUP
1 shake WORCESTERSHIRE SAUCE
splash WHITE WINE (optional)
1/2 soup can MILK

STEP 1: In skillet, on medium high heat, fry chops in hot oil till brown on each side. Lay onion slices over meat.

STEP 2: Stir rest of ingredients together in small bowl till smooth; spoon over meat and onions.

STEP 3: Cover. When mixture starts to bubble, reduce heat to lowest setting and continue cooking 30 minutes.

footnote: Cook pork until there is no pink coloring in the meat when you cut through it.

SAUCY PORK CHOPS

35 MIN.

1 TO 2 SERVINGS

MEATY MEALS

SKILLET WITH LID TOP OF STOVE

MEDIUM HIGH TO LOWEST HEAT

SAUSAGE, KRAUT & APPLESAUCE

15 MIN.

1 TO 2 SERVINGS

SKILLET WITH LID
TOP OF STOVE

MEDIUM HEAT

NEED:
1 large fully cooked POLISH SAUSAGE
1 8 oz. can SAUERKRAUT
couple spoonfuls APPLESAUCE
spoonful BROWN SUGAR

STEP 1: Place sausage in skillet.

STEP 2: Add sauerkraut, applesauce and brown sugar. Stir to mix.

STEP 3: Cover and cook on medium heat till hot (approximately 10–15 minutes).

footnote: Goes well with boiled potatoes and green salad.

NEED:
- 1 lb. STEWING BEEF
- 1/2 pkg. DRY ONION SOUP MIX
- 1 4 oz. can MUSHROOMS, undrained
- 1 cup CREAM OF MUSHROOM soup
- 1/4 cup SHERRY

Preheat oven to 325°

In deep ovenproof pan, stir together all ingredients. Cover tightly and bake in 325° oven for 2½ to 3 hours. Stir a couple of times during cooking, if you can.

footnote: Serve over hot rice. Makes its own gravy. Tastes "gourmet."

MEATY MEALS

DEEP OVENPROOF PAN WITH LID

325° OVEN

TAMALE & CHEESE DINNER

5 MIN.

1 TO 2 SERVINGS

MEATY MEALS

SKILLET WITH LID
TOP OF STOVE

LOW HEAT

NEED:
1 can TAMALES
1 8 oz. can CORN, drained
Handful grated CHEDDAR CHEESE

STEP 1: Unwrap tamales and break into pieces. Lay in skillet.

STEP 2: Top tamales with corn and sprinkle with cheese.

STEP 3: Cover with lid and cook on low heat 5 minutes or till hot.

footnote: Top with sliced avocado and spoonful cottage cheese or sour cream.

NEED:

1 clove GARLIC, mashed
1 small ONION, chopped
1/2 lb. GROUND BEEF
1 tablespoon VEGETABLE OIL
1 16 oz. can WHOLE ITALIAN TOMATOES, cut up
1 15 oz. can TOMATO SAUCE
1 6 oz. can TOMATO PASTE
splash BURGUNDY WINE
1 teaspoon SALT
1 tablespoon ITALIAN HERB SEASONING

STEP 1: In large saucepan, on medium heat, brown garlic and onion in hot oil. Add ground beef. Stir and cook till crumbly and browned. (Drain off grease into an old can, not down drain.)

STEP 2: Stir in rest of ingredients. When mixture comes to a boil, turn heat down to lowest setting. Cover tightly.

STEP 3: Cook slowly at least 1 hour. (Longer cooking enhances flavor.) Stir occasionally.

Serve on hot pasta.

THAT'S ITALIAN SPAGHETTI SAUCE

1¼ HOURS (OR LONGER)

MEATY MEALS

SAUCEPAN WITH LID TOP OF STOVE

MEDIUM TO LOWEST HEAT

Roasted Pumpkin Seeds.

Scoop out seeds. Wash seeds and remove any pulp.

Dry overnight on paper towels.

Melt couple tablespoons margarine and mix with seeds.

Spread on ungreased cookie sheet or foil.

Sprinkle with salt.

Bake slowly in 250° oven for 2 hours, stirring several times.

VEGETABLES

NEED:

1 medium POTATO, washed (leave skin on)
VEGETABLE OIL
handful shredded CHEDDAR CHEESE

STEP 1: Slice potato into 1/4 inch slices.

STEP 2: Lay slices on broiler pan rack. Brush each slice lightly with oil.

STEP 3: Broil till brown. Turn potatoes over, brush with oil and broil till brown. Sprinkle with cheese and broil a few more minutes till cheese melts.

footnote: Top with sour cream, bacon bits and chives. Makes a great snack.

BROILED POTATO SLICES

10 MIN.

SEVERAL SERVINGS

VEGETABLES

BROILER PAN & RACK

BROIL (HIGHEST HEAT IN OVEN)

COOKED FRESH SPINACH

10 MIN.

1 TO 2 SERVINGS

SAUCEPAN WITH LID TOP OF STOVE

MEDIUM LOW HEAT

NEED:
1 bunch SPINACH
1/4 LEMON
1 tablespoon MARGARINE
SALT, PEPPER to taste

STEP 1: Wash spinach. The easy way: fill sink with water and dump loose spinach in. Break off stems at root, holding under water. (Both spinach leaves and stems are tasty.)

STEP 2: Shake off excess water and stuff spinach into saucepan. Add couple spoonfuls of water. Cover and cook at medium low heat 5 to 10 minutes or till tender.

STEP 3: Drain spinach and squeeze lemon on. Add margarine, salt and pepper to taste.

footnote: Use whole bunch—it shrinks when cooked.

NEED:

    1 8 oz. can PORK AND BEANS
    1 spoonful BROWN SUGAR
    1 plop CATSUP
    1 tablespoon chopped ONION
    dab MUSTARD

STEP 1: Stir all ingredients together in small saucepan. Cook on medium heat till beans start to boil.

STEP 2: Reduce heat to lowest setting. Cover. Cook 10 minutes to blend flavors.

footnote: Can be cooked longer to enhance flavors.

VEGETABLES

**SAUCEPAN WITH LID
TOP OF STOVE**

**MEDIUM TO LOWEST
HEAT**

MOM'S MASHED POTATOES

25 MIN.

1 TO 2 SERVINGS

SAUCEPAN AND LID
TOP OF STOVE

MEDIUM HEAT

NEED:
2 POTATOES (white, red or russet will do)
BUTTER or MARGARINE
MILK
SALT, PEPPER to taste

STEP 1: Wash and peel potatoes. Cut into quarters. Place in large saucepan. Cover with cold water. Cover with lid and cook on medium heat 20 minutes or till potatoes fall apart when you poke them with fork.

STEP 2: Remove from heat and drain potatoes in pan using lid to keep potatoes from falling out of pan. Set pan on counter and mash potatoes with fork (or, even better, with an electric mixer if you have one). Add a couple of pats of butter and about 1/4 cup milk. Keep beating with fork or mixer till potatoes are light and fluffy. Salt and pepper to taste. Top with pat of butter.

PEAS IN SNOW

5 MIN.

1 SERVING

NEED:

    1 small package FROZEN PEAS, quick-thawed (see footnote)
    2 large tablespoons MAYONNAISE
    3 large tablespoons SOUR CREAM
    dash GARLIC SALT
    1 HARD-COOKED EGG, chopped
    juice of 1 LEMON

STEP 1: Combine all ingredients in saucepan and stir gently.

STEP 2: Heat on low heat 5 minutes, stirring often. Don't let it boil!!

footnote: To quick-thaw frozen peas: Run cold water over peas in strainer 1 minute. If you don't have a strainer, use saucepan and drain with pan lid tilted slightly to let only the water drain out. Make sure all water is out of pan before using recipe.

This is an excellent and cheap meal when used as a topping over a baked potato or boiled red potatoes.

**SAUCEPAN
TOP OF STOVE**

LOW HEAT

SPANISH RICE

20 MIN.

1 TO 2 SERVINGS

**SKILLET
TOP OF STOVE**

**HIGH TO LOWEST
HEAT**

NEED:
2 tablespoons VEGETABLE OIL
1 ONION, chopped
1/2 GREEN BELL PEPPER, chopped
1 5 oz. can TOMATO SAUCE
1 can WATER (use empty tomato sauce can)
spoonful SALSA
dash SALT, PEPPER
1/2 cup RICE (uncooked)

STEP 1: Heat oil in skillet on high heat. Add onion and bell pepper. Stir and cook till onion is limp.

STEP 2: Stir in rest of ingredients. When mixture starts to boil, turn heat to lowest setting. Cover and cook about 18 minutes or till liquid is absorbed.

NEED:
1–2 ears fresh CORN ON COB
pat BUTTER or MARGARINE
SALT, PEPPER to taste

STEP 1: Tear off and discard outer husk on corn. Pick off any strands of "silk" remaining on ear of corn. Wash corn under cold water.

STEP 2: Put cold water in pan to 1 inch deep. Turn heat to high and bring water to boiling.

STEP 3: Lay corn in pan of boiling water. (If corn is too long, break so that corn lies flat in pan.) Cover pan and steam on high heat 5 minutes. Carefully remove corn. Spread hot corn with butter, salt and pepper.

footnote: When buying corn, peel back husk and look for white or pale-yellow corn. Dark-gold corn can be tough when cooked.

VEGETABLES

LARGE SAUCEPAN WITH LID TOP OF STOVE

HIGH HEAT

SWEET CARROTS

10 MIN.

1 SERVING

SAUCEPAN WITH LID
TOP OF STOVE

MEDIUM HEAT

NEED:

    2-3 CARROTS, washed and scraped
    2 tablespoons BUTTER or MARGARINE
    2 tablespoons BROWN SUGAR

STEP 1: Cut carrots into quarters lengthwise. Lay carrots in small saucepan and just cover with water. Turn heat to high. When water starts to boil, cover with lid and turn heat to medium. Boil gently 8 minutes or till carrots are just barely tender. Drain water from pan.

STEP 2: In same pan, add butter and brown sugar to carrots. Stir very gently and heat on medium heat 1 minute. Sauce will be bubbly and syrupy.

NEED:

1 tablespoon BUTTER or MARGARINE
1/2 teaspoon MUSTARD
quick splash WORCESTERSHIRE SAUCE
SALT, PEPPER to taste
1 8 oz. can CUT GREEN BEANS, drained
couple spoonfuls CORN FLAKES, crushed

STEP 1: Melt butter in saucepan. Stir in mustard and Worcestershire sauce.

STEP 2: Stir green beans into sauce. Heat on low heat till hot 1 to 2 minutes.

STEP 3: Sprinkle corn flake crumbs over and serve.

footnote: Try topping with spoonful of egg salad.

TANGY GREEN BEANS

5 MIN.

1 TO 2 SERVINGS

VEGETABLES

SAUCEPAN TOP OF STOVE

LOW HEAT

ZUCCHINI & TOMATOES

15 MIN.

1 TO 2 SERVINGS

SKILLET
TOP OF STOVE

MEDIUM TO LOWEST HEAT

NEED:
2-3 slices BACON, cut up before cooking
1/2 ONION, chopped
1 2 oz. can SLICED MUSHROOMS
1/2 small can TOMATOES or 2 fresh TOMATOES, cut up
2 ZUCCHINI, sliced in rounds
grated PARMESAN CHEESE

STEP 1: In skillet, on medium heat, cook bacon with onion and mushrooms till bacon is done. Drain off grease (into an old can—not down the drain).

STEP 2: Add cut up tomatoes and zucchini. Cook on lowest heat approximately 10 minutes or till zucchini is tender.

STEP 3: Sprinkle with Parmesan cheese and serve.

footnote: Try adding chopped green bell peppers, carrots or green beans to Step 2.

MUSHROOMS—2 oz. can, drained and lightly cooked in 1 tablespoon margarine.

LEMON BUTTER—squeeze 1/2 lemon into 1 tablespoon hot melted margarine

CHEDDAR CHEESE—grated over hot vegetables

EASY HOLLANDAISE—cook in small saucepan, on low heat:
  2 spoonfuls SOUR CREAM
  2 spoonfuls MAYONNAISE
  dab MUSTARD
  1 spoonful LEMON JUICE

TANGY SAUCE—stir together and pour over vegetables:
  1 tablespoon hot MARGARINE
  1 teaspoon MUSTARD
  squirt WORCESTERSHIRE SAUCE
  squirt LEMON JUICE

MISC. UTENSILS

HANDY HINT

Reheating meats will be faster and save your pans from burning if you add a small amount of water (1/4 cup) to pan first, add meat, cover and heat on medium heat till hot.

If meat has been defrosted, DON'T REFREEZE it unless it has been cooked.

USING LEFTOVERS

USING LEFTOVERS

BEEF — use in:
Meaty Fried Rice (p. 130)
Quick Minestrone Soup (p. 24)
Yesterday's Roast Beef (p. 132)

BREAD — use in:
Easy Cheesy Fondue (p. 138)
French Toast (p. 6)
Tuna Soufflé (p. 82)

CHICKEN OR TURKEY — use in:
All in One Casserole (p. 124)
Eggs Foo Yung (p. 125)
Leftover Chicken & Potato Bake (p. 128)
Meaty Fried Rice (p. 130)
Quick Minestrone Soup (p. 24)

HAM AND PORK — use in:
All in One Casserole (p. 124)
EZ Cheese Sauce (p. 126)
Ham on Buns (p. 127)
Leftover Ham Stew (p. 129)
Meaty Fried Rice (p. 130)
Omelets (p. 5)

MACARONI, RICE AND PASTA — use in:
Meaty Fried Rice (p. 130)
Reheating Directions (p. 131)
Reheat and use with:
Cheap Roast (p. 92)
EZ Cheese Sauce (p. 126)
Gizzards in Gravy (p. 68)
Meatless Spaghetti Sauce (p. 55)
Pork Chops à l'Orange (p. 99)
Sherried Beef (p. 103)
That's Italian Spaghetti Sauce (p. 105)

VEGETABLES — use in:
All in One Casserole (p. 124)
Basic Stir-Fry (p. 53)
EZ Cheese Sauce (p. 126)
Leftover Chicken & Potato Bake (p. 128)
Leftover Ham Stew (p. 129)
Quick Minestrone Soup (p. 24)
Vegetable Toppings (p. 119)

ALL IN ONE CASSEROLE

40 MIN.

2 TO 3 SERVINGS

OVENPROOF BAKING DISH

375° OVEN

124

NEED:
- 1 cup CHEDDAR CHEESE, shredded
- 1 small package FROZEN CHOPPED SPINACH, thawed (or any leftover cooked green vegetable)
- 1 ONION, chopped
- 1 cup cooked HAM or CHICKEN, cut in small pieces (or you can use canned tuna, shrimp, crab, chicken, etc., drained well)
- 1½ cups MILK
- 3/4 cup BAKING MIX (e.g., Bisquick)
- 3 EGGS
- 1/2 teaspoon SALT, dash PEPPER

Preheat oven to 375°

STEP 1: Squeeze all liquid out of spinach and lay spinach in bottom of shallow baking dish. Top with layer of meat, onion, then cheese.

STEP 2: Combine in blender jar milk, baking mix, eggs, salt and pepper. Blend on medium speed 1 minute. Pour over layered casserole.

STEP 3: Bake in 375° oven 30 to 40 minutes (or till knife inserted comes out dry). Remove and let cool for a few minutes.

footnote: This makes enough to have next day. Even tastes good cold.

NEED:

4 EGGS
dash SALT and PEPPER
1 tablespoon VEGETABLE OIL
couple MUSHROOMS, chopped small
couple WATER CHESTNUTS, chopped small
1 stalk CELERY, chopped small
handful fresh BEAN SPROUTS
splash SOY SAUCE
handful COOKED CHICKEN, finely chopped

STEP 1: In large bowl, beat with fork eggs, salt and pepper till blended. Then add rest of ingredients (except oil). Stir well.

STEP 2: Heat oil in skillet on medium high heat. Spoon mixture onto hot skillet. (Make about size of pancake.)

STEP 3: Turn over when underside is brown. Cook till eggs are set.

footnote: Heat 12 oz. can mushroom gravy and pour over.

EGGS FOO YUNG

10 MIN.

1 TO 2 SERVINGS

USING LEFTOVERS

**LARGE BOWL &
SKILLET
TOP OF STOVE**

MEDIUM HIGH HEAT

EZ
CHEESE
SAUCE

5 MIN.

SEVERAL SERVINGS

USING LEFTOVERS

SAUCEPAN
TOP OF STOVE

MEDIUM LOW HEAT

NEED:
    1 can WHITE SAUCE (in soup or condiment section of market)
    handful CHEDDAR CHEESE, grated
    2 HARD-COOKED EGGS, chopped

In saucepan, on medium low heat, stir and heat white sauce and cheese till cheese melts. Add eggs. Stir and use.

USES:
- Serve over noodles, vegetables or meat
- Toast, slice of ham, top with EZ Cheese Sauce
- Omit the eggs and use over omelets

NEED:

    1 tablespoon MARGARINE
    1/4 ONION, chopped
    1/8 GREEN BELL PEPPER, chopped small
    3 EGGS
    splash MILK
    handful COOKED HAM, chopped small
    SALT, PEPPER to taste
    2 KAISER ROLLS or HAMBURGER BUNS

STEP 1: In skillet, on medium heat, melt margarine. Add onion and bell pepper. Cook 3 min.

STEP 2: In small bowl, stir together eggs, milk, ham and seasonings. Beat lightly with fork.

STEP 3: Pour into skillet. Cook and stir till egg is done to your liking.

Serve over toasted buns!

HAM ON BUNS

10 MIN.

1 TO 2 SERVINGS

USING LEFTOVERS

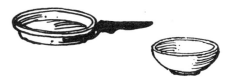

SMALL BOWL & SKILLET TOP OF STOVE

MEDIUM HEAT

LEFTOVER CHICKEN & POTATO BAKE

40 MIN.

1 TO 2 SERVINGS

OVEN BAKING DISH

350° OVEN

NEED:
>1 medium POTATO, peeled and sliced
>handful cooked CHICKEN or TURKEY, bite-size pieces
>1/2 medium ONION, sliced
>1/2 can CREAM OF CELERY soup (or whatever cream-style soup you have)
>1/4 cup MILK

Preheat oven to 350°

STEP 1: In oven baking dish arrange layers of potato, chicken and onion.

STEP 2: Mix together soup and milk in small bowl. Pour over top of layers.

STEP 3: Cover. Bake in 350° oven for 40 minutes or till potatoes are tender when you poke them with a fork.

footnote: Try using leftover cooked potatoes and shorten baking time to 20 minutes.

NEED:
- 1 handful COOKED HAM, bite-size pieces
- 1 can CREAM OF POTATO SOUP
- 1/4 soup can MILK
- handful leftover COOKED VEGETABLES
- splash WHITE WINE (optional)
- couple shakes PARMESAN CHEESE

STEP 1: In saucepan, dump in all ingredients except Parmesan cheese. Stir.

STEP 2: Heat on medium heat just till starts to boil; immediately turn down heat to lowest setting. Cook 10 minutes, stirring often to keep milk from sticking.

STEP 3: Add Parmesan cheese, stirring till melted.

footnote: If you like it spicy, add a dash of Tabasco™ sauce.

LEFTOVER HAM STEW

10 MIN.

1 TO 2 SERVINGS

USING LEFTOVERS

SAUCEPAN TOP OF STOVE

MEDIUM TO LOW HEAT

MEATY FRIED RICE

15 MIN.

1 TO 2 SERVINGS

**SKILLET
TOP OF STOVE**

**HIGH TO MEDIUM
HEAT**

NEED:
1 tablespoon MARGARINE
2 EGGS
1 tablespoon VEGETABLE OIL
1 GREEN ONION, thinly sliced
1 cup COLD COOKED RICE
handful any leftover cooked MEAT, chopped small
tablespoon SOY SAUCE

STEP 1: In skillet, on medium heat, melt margarine and lightly scramble eggs. Remove eggs from skillet and set on plate till later.

STEP 2: In same skillet, heat oil on high heat till very hot. Add green onion and stir 1 minute. Lower heat to medium. Add rice and meat. Stir and fry till meat and rice are hot (approximately 2 minutes).

STEP 3: Add soy sauce and scrambled eggs. Stir and fry 1 more minute.

REHEATING MACARONI, RICE OR PASTA

5 MIN.

ANY NUMBER OF SERVINGS

SAUCEPAN WITH LID TOP OF STOVE

MEDIUM HEAT

1. Dump leftover cooked macaroni, rice or pasta into saucepan.

2. Add couple spoonfuls water. Cover tightly. Heat on medium heat a couple of minutes or till hot.

3. Drain off any excess water, then use.

YESTERDAY'S ROAST BEEF

10 MIN.

1 TO 2 SERVINGS

USING LEFTOVERS

**SKILLET
TOP OF STOVE**

**MEDIUM TO LOW
HEAT**

NEED:
  1/2 ONION, chopped
  1 tablespoon MARGARINE
  1 tablespoon FLOUR
  1 cup BEEF BROTH (use INSTANT BEEF BOUILLON, dissolved in hot
    water)
  1/2 cup RED WINE
  couple shakes WORCESTERSHIRE SAUCE
  4 slices leftover cooked ROAST BEEF

STEP 1: In skillet, on medium heat, cook onion in margarine till golden. Quickly stir in flour. Reduce heat to low.

STEP 2: Add beef broth to skillet slowly. Stir till well mixed with flour and onion. Stir in wine and Worcestershire sauce.

STEP 3: Lay beef slices in sauce and heat thoroughly (approximately 5 minutes).

Burned Pots and Pans? Spray pans with oven cleaner (following oven cleaner directions on can). Let pans sit overnight and they will be easier to clean.
DO NOT USE ON PANS WITH NON-STICK COATING.

Quickie Cookie: Lay a marshmallow on a graham cracker. Set on a
sheet of aluminum foil. Heat under broiler just till marshmallow melts
and gets brown and bubbly.

SNACKS & PARTY FOODS

NEED:
   1 15 oz. can TOMATOES, cut up (not Italian style)
   1 15 oz. can THICK CHUNKY TOMATO SAUCE
   1 fresh TOMATO, chopped small
   1 ONION, chopped
   1/2 GREEN BELL PEPPER, chopped
   1 clove GARLIC, mashed (or garlic salt)
   1 teaspoon fresh JALAPEÑO PEPPER, chopped very fine (use
      according to taste)

Dump all ingredients in a large bowl. Stir to mix well. Cover and place in refrigerator.

footnote: Tastes best when allowed to chill for a few hours to let flavors blend.

SNACKS & PARTY FOODS

LARGE BOWL

NO COOKING

EASY CHEESY FONDUE

5 MIN.

SEVERAL SERVINGS

SAUCEPAN
TOP OF STOVE

MEDIUM LOW HEAT

NEED:
- 2 tablespoons MARGARINE
- 2 tablespoons FLOUR
- 1 cup MILK
- 1 teaspoon MUSTARD
- 2 handfuls shredded CHEDDAR CHEESE
- FRENCH BREAD, cut into bite-size chunks

STEP 1: In saucepan, on medium low heat, melt margarine and stir in flour till well mixed and smooth.

STEP 2: Slowly add milk. Stir and heat till thick. Add mustard and cheese, stirring till melted.

footnote: Dip chunks of French bread into cheese sauce using forks.

NEED:

1 8 oz. jar PROCESSED CHEESE SPREAD
4 GREEN ONIONS, finely chopped
1/2 GREEN BELL PEPPER, finely chopped
dash PAPRIKA (in spice section of market)
1 tablespoon WORCESTERSHIRE SAUCE
1 7 oz. can MINCED CLAMS, drained well

In saucepan, on low heat, mix all ingredients together. Stir and heat till cheese melts.

USES:

Fantastic as a sauce over linguini pasta
Serve hot with chips
Dunk bite-size pieces of French bread

HOT CLAMS & CHEESE

10 MIN.

SEVERAL SERVINGS

SNACKS & PARTY FOODS

SAUCEPAN
TOP OF STOVE

LOW HEAT

FRESH FRUIT DIP

3 MIN.

SEVERAL SERVINGS

SMALL BOWL

NO COOKING

Blend in small bowl:
    2 spoonfuls BROWN SUGAR
    8 oz. carton SOUR CREAM

Use as a dip for FRESH FRUIT:

- WATERMELON CHUNKS
- STRAWBERRIES
- BANANA CHUNKS
- PINEAPPLE SPEARS
- APPLE WEDGES
- PEAR SLICES

NEED:
- 1/4 cup MARGARINE
- 2 cups WHOLE PEANUTS or ALMONDS, shelled
- 1 teaspoon CHILI POWDER
- 1 teaspoon GARLIC SALT

STEP 1: Melt margarine in skillet on high heat. Add rest of ingredients to hot margarine and stir to mix well.

STEP 2: Cook and stir on medium heat about 5 minutes or till nuts turn golden brown.

STEP 3: Empty nuts out of skillet over paper towels on large plate to cool.

SKILLET
TOP OF STOVE

HIGH TO MEDIUM
HEAT

footnote: Great snack hot or cooled. Can be stored in airtight container when cooled.

PATTY'S DEVILED EGGS

10 MIN.

SEVERAL SERVINGS

SMALL BOWL

NO COOKING

NEED:
6 HARD-COOKED EGGS
2 tablespoons MAYONNAISE
1/2 teaspoon MUSTARD
couple dashes each CELERY SALT, GARLIC SALT, PEPPER
1 small can baby shrimp (optional but sure tastes good)
PARSLEY and PAPRIKA (optional)

STEP 1: Cut eggs in half, lengthwise. Scoop out yolks (yellow part) and put in small mixing bowl. (Put white halves aside to be filled later.) Add mayonnaise, mustard, celery salt, garlic salt and pepper to yolks. Mash and stir together till everything is well mixed, smooth and creamy.

STEP 2: If using shrimp, stir very gently into mixture.

STEP 3: Spoon mixture into egg-white halves. Sprinkle tops of yolks with paprika and parsley. Lay on attractive platter and place in refrigerator till time to serve.

footnote: Better hide them with aluminum foil or they may just disappear before your party.

- **DILL DIP**

NEED:
>1 cup MAYONNAISE
>1 8 oz. carton SOUR CREAM
>2 GREEN ONIONS, sliced thin
>1½ teaspoons DILL WEED (in spice section of market)
>1½ teaspoons SEASONED SALT

Blend all together in bowl and chill. Serve with raw vegetables.

- **DEVILISH DIP**

NEED:
>1 8 oz. carton SOUR CREAM
>4¼ oz. can DEVILED HAM SPREAD
>dash WORCESTERSHIRE SAUCE

Blend together and chill.

SNACKS & PARTY FOODS

SMALL BOWL

NO COOKING

PIGS IN A BLANKET

15 MIN.

MAKES 8 SMALL ROLLS

SKILLET & ALUMINUM FOIL

350° OVEN

NEED:
   1 can refrigerated CRESCENT ROLLS
   1 pkg. SAUSAGE LINKS (brown and serve type, skinless)

Preheat oven to 350°

STEP 1: Cook sausages according to directions on package. Remove sausages and drain on paper towel.

STEP 2: Roll sausages into uncooked crescent rolls, follow directions for rolling on package. Place on cookie sheet or aluminum foil and bake in 350° oven 10 minutes or till golden.

NEED:

1/4 ONION, chopped
1 tablespoon MARGARINE
1/8 GREEN BELL PEPPER, chopped
1/2 can TOMATO SOUP
1 tablespoon BROWN SUGAR
dash WORCESTERSHIRE SAUCE
quick dash VINEGAR
dab MUSTARD
4–5 WIENERS, cut into bite-size pieces

STEP 1: In skillet, on medium heat, cook onion in margarine till onion is transparent.

STEP 2: Dump in other ingredients, except wieners. Stir well to blend flavors.

STEP 3: Add wieners and heat on low heat 2 minutes or till wieners are hot.

footnote: Serve in a heatproof dish and set on a hot plate. Be sure to have toothpicks nearby for skewers.

SAUCY BARBECUED FRANKS

8 MIN.

SEVERAL SERVINGS

SNACKS & PARTY FOODS

SKILLET
TOP OF STOVE

MEDIUM TO LOW
HEAT

If you don't have a punch bowl, use the kitchen sink—washed first, please.

When recipe calls for part of package of dry onion soup, use the rest mixed with sour cream as a dip.

DRINKS & DESSERTS

NEED:

2 6 oz. cans FROZEN ORANGE JUICE
1 6 oz. can FROZEN LEMONADE
1½ quarts ICE WATER
2 quarts CHAMPAGNE (well chilled)
ORANGE SLICES (chilled)

STEP 1: Dilute orange juice and lemonade with ice water in punch bowl.

STEP 2: Just before serving, gently pour champagne into punch bowl.

STEP 3: Float thin orange slices in bowl. Serve.

footnote: Just before serving, try adding 1 pint orange sherbet to punch.

DRINKS & DESSERTS

PUNCH BOWL

NO COOKING

149

CHOCOLATE COFFEE

10 MIN.

ANY NUMBER SERVINGS

COFFEE MUGS

NEED:
BREWED HOT COFFEE
HOT CHOCOLATE
WHIPPED TOPPING
FRESH ORANGE PEEL, grated

STEP 1: Stir together in large mugs equal amounts hot coffee and hot chocolate.

STEP 2: Top with whipped topping and sprinkle with some grated orange peel.

NEED:
QUART JAR with tight-fitting lid
CRUSHED ICE
1/2 LEMON
spoonful SUGAR or LOW-CAL SWEETENER

STEP 1: Fill jar 2/3 full with crushed ice. Add water till almost to top of jar.

STEP 2: Squeeze lemon in. Sprinkle sugar on top.

STEP 3: Close lid tightly. Shake vigorously. Open and drink! Cool and refreshing!

LEMON AID

2 MIN.

1 SERVING

DRINKS & DESSERTS

QUART JAR WITH LID

NO COOKING

LET'S PARTY PUNCH

5 MIN.

12 SERVINGS (1 CUP EACH)

DRINKS & DESSERTS

LARGE BOWL OR LEAK-PROOF SINK

NO COOKING

NEED:
- 2 liters BURGUNDY or ROSÉ WINE (chilled)
- 1 quart APPLE JUICE
- juice 1/4 LEMON
- 1 cup SUGAR
- 1 quart GINGER ALE (chilled)
- ICE CUBES (1 tray)

STEP 1: Mix all ingredients in bowl, stirring to dissolve sugar.

STEP 2: Add ice cubes.

STEP 3: Serve at once.

NEED:
COFFEE
7 WHOLE CLOVES
1 STICK CINNAMON
3 large spoonfuls SUGAR
WHIPPED TOPPING

STEP 1: Before brewing six cups coffee in coffeemaker, add cloves, cinnamon and sugar to dry coffee grounds in basket.

STEP 2: Perk coffee as usual. Pour in mugs.

STEP 3: Top off each mug of coffee with a plop of whipped topping.

DRINKS & DESSERTS

COFFEEMAKER

CHOCOLATE PEARS PLUS

3 MIN.

1 SERVING

SMALL SERVING DISH

NO COOKING

154

NEED:
> PEAR HALF
> VANILLA ICE CREAM or FROZEN YOGURT
> CHOCOLATE TOPPING

STEP 1: Place a pear half in bottom of small glass bowl.

STEP 2: Top with ice cream or frozen yogurt.

STEP 3: Drizzle hot or cold chocolate topping over.

Try same recipe using VANILLA ICE CREAM or YOGURT and:

PEACHES and BUTTERSCOTCH TOPPING
HALVED BANANA and PINEAPPLE TOPPING
HALF CANTALOUPE and spoonful BROWN SUGAR

NEED:
  1/2 cup PEANUT BUTTER
  1/2 cup HONEY
  1 cup WHEAT GERM
  SHREDDED COCONUT or CHOPPED NUTS

STEP 1: In bowl, blend peanut butter, honey, wheat germ together. Roll into small balls (see footnote.)

STEP 2: Roll balls in coconut or nuts. Refrigerate.

Eat when chilled and hardened.

footnote: To keep candy from sticking to your hands, rub a little butter on your fingers first.

JUST A TRIFLE

10 MIN.

SEVERAL SERVINGS

DEEP GLASS BOWL (a fancy one if you have it)

NO COOKING

NEED:

1 10 oz. POUND CAKE, cut into 8 slices
1/4 cup SHERRY or PORT
1 cup fresh or frozen BERRIES
4 tablespoons BERRY JAM or PRESERVES
1 6 oz. package INSTANT VANILLA PUDDING—make according to directions and set aside
1 small carton FROZEN WHIPPED TOPPING (e.g., Cool Whip), thawed and stirred with a spoon.

STEP 1: Arrange half the cake slices along bottom and sides of bowl. Spoon half the sherry over cake.

STEP 2: Sprinkle half the berries over cake and top with 2 tablespoons jam. Pour half the pudding over all.

STEP 3: Repeat Steps 1 and 2 using remaining half of ingredients (except whipped topping). Then spoon softened whipped topping over trifle and refrigerate overnight.

footnote: Best to make this absolutely gorgeous dessert one day ahead in order to let flavors blend together.

NEED:
- 1 small box LEMON or LIME SUGAR-FREE GELATIN
- 3/4 cup BOILING WATER
- 12 ICE CUBES
- 1 cup LOW-CAL WHIPPED TOPPING, softened to room temperature
- several thin slices of fresh LIMES or LEMONS
- 1 8-inch PIE CRUST, baked and cooled

STEP 1: In large mixing bowl, add boiling water to gelatin mix and stir 2 minutes. Add ice cubes, one at a time, and stir another 2 minutes. Gelatin should be starting to thicken.

STEP 2: Gently stir in whipped topping. Stir till well blended and smooth. Pour into baked and cooled pie crust. Refrigerate for several hours before cutting.

footnote: Fancy it up by adding thin lemon slices on top of pie before serving.

NO-COOK PUDDINGS

5 MIN.

SEVERAL SERVINGS

DESSERT DISH

NO COOKING

Make pudding according to directions on package of INSTANT PUDDING MIX, then add to:

- **BUTTERSCOTCH** —couple drops BRANDY
- **CHOCOLATE** —spoonful CHOCOLATE CHIPS
  - or —spoonful MALTED MILK
  - or —spoonful PEANUT BUTTER
- **LEMON** —couple drops fresh LEMON JUICE
- **VANILLA** —spoonful WALNUTS; SHREDDED COCONUT

NEED:
    Unsliced FRESH BREAD (best if fresh from a bakery)
    BUTTER or MARGARINE
    GRANULATED SUGAR
    LEMON CURD (this is the stuff used as cake fillings) or RED BERRY
      JAM

STEP 1: Slice fresh bread and spread liberally with butter.

STEP 2: Sprinkle sugar over and shake off excess.

STEP 3: Spread on lemon curd or jam.

Now, slice in quarters, put on a pretty plate, sit down with a cold glass of milk and enjoy. Yum!!

POOR FOLKS' DESSERTS

1 MIN.

SEVERAL SERVINGS

DRINKS & DESSERTS

SHARP KNIFE

NO COOKING

QUICK BAKED APPLES

20 MIN.

1 TO 2 SERVINGS

DRINKS & DESSERTS

SAUCEPAN WITH LID TOP OF STOVE

MEDIUM TO LOW HEAT

NEED:
- 2 LARGE BAKING APPLES (MACINTOSH, ROME BEAUTY)
- 2 small spoonfuls SUGAR
- dab MARGARINE
- dash CINNAMON
- 1/2 cup WATER

STEP 1: Wash apples and scoop out cores (don't go through the bottom of the apples). In center hole of each apple, pour sugar till almost full. Dab with margarine and sprinkle cinnamon on top.

STEP 2: Pour water in saucepan. Gently place apples in water. Cover.

STEP 3: Turn heat to medium and bring water to boiling point. Lower heat and cook apples till tender (approximately 20 minutes).

footnote: Serve with warm milk or ice.

NEED:

2 16 oz. cans SLICED PEACHES with juice
1 pkg. YELLOW CAKE MIX
1 stick MARGARINE (or 1/2 cup)
1 cup CHOPPED NUTS

STEP 1: Spread peaches and juice in bottom of baking dish

STEP 2: Sprinkle dry cake mix on top of peaches. Dot with margarine. Sprinkle nuts on top.

STEP 3: Bake 45 minutes in 350˚ oven or till cobbler is golden.

footnote: Serve warm with ice cream.

SIMPLE PEACH COBBLER

45 MIN.

SEVERAL SERVINGS

DRINKS & DESSERTS

13" X 9" OVEN BAKING DISH

350˚ OVEN

STRAWBERRY DELIGHT PIE

10 MIN.

6 SLICES

NO COOKING

NEED:

3 oz. pkg. STRAWBERRY GELATIN
2/3 cup BOILING WATER
14 ICE CUBES
1 8 oz. carton small curd COTTAGE CHEESE
1 BANANA, sliced
GRAHAM CRACKER CRUST, premade (in baking mix section of market)

STEP 1: Dissolve gelatin in boiling water in large bowl. Stir 3 minutes. Add ice cubes and stir 2 more minutes. (Gelatin will be thick.) Remove excess ice cubes.

STEP 2: Add cottage cheese and stir well to blend.

STEP 3: Lay banana slices in bottom of pie crust. Spoon gelatin mix over bananas and chill 1 hour before cutting.

INDEX